25 Super-Fun Math Spinner Games

Easy-to-Assemble, Fun-to-Play Games to Develop Mathematical Thinking

By Judi Aronson

SCHOLASTIC
PROFESSIONAL BOOKS

NEW YORK • TORONTO • LONDON • AUCKLAND • SYDNEY

ACKNOWLEDGMENTS

For my parents Ilus and Sanyi who taught me the importance of taking risks. For my children Danielle and David who continue to teach me new lessons every day. For my husband and partner Howard who has always supported me. And for the many teachers who have inspired me and who make a difference in children's lives everyday.

Cover design by Vincent Ceci and Jaime Lucero
Interior Design by Solutions by Design

ISBN: 0-590-34138-3

Contents

25 SUPER-FUN MATH SPINNER GAMES
Scholastic Professional Books, 1997

Introduction

Change in the teaching of mathematics is needed because the world is changing. Recent technological advances, and a world that is becoming more complex and quantitative, make mathematical thinking even more important. The National Council of Teachers of Mathematics (NCTM) has published documents to establish a framework for the transformation of the teaching and learning of mathematics. *The Curriculum and Evaluation Standards for School Mathematics* (1989) suggests that we make mathematics come alive for our students by encouraging classroom opportunities that develop effective problem-solving skills and positive attitudes toward math.

BENEFIT OF MATH SPINNER GAMES

Currently, many mathematics curricula do not include opportunities for students to appreciate the useful, fun, and creative aspects of mathematics (NCTM, 1989). The spinner games in this book show students that learning math can be fun and encourage them to value mathematics, one of the major goals of the NCTM standards. Many of these math spinner games use cooperative learning techniques and encourage positive social experiences between students. Students will find themselves communicating about mathematical concepts during any one of these games. Using mathematical language, a major part of the NCTM Standards, is important for helping students understand and clarify concepts and develop reasoning skills. When students become engrossed in these math games, the critical thinking and social skills they are using can give mathematics a whole new excitement. These games develop a wide range of skills—inductive and deductive reasoning, brainstorming, observing, experimenting with different solutions, working together in groups, and written and verbal expression. Spinners enable students to experience probability. General ideas about what is certain, impossible, more likely, or less likely emerge by using spinners.

As students play these games, they discover ways of arriving at solutions that can be applied to a multitude of problems, mathematical or otherwise. In this way, spinner games provide students with self-confidence in their ability to apply mathematical knowledge to new situations and start them on the road to developing the thinking skills of tomorrow's adults.

USING SPINNER GAMES

These spinner games are highly motivational and can be used effectively to practice and reinforce specific math skills. They can be used before a lesson to introduce a new concept or after the lesson as an extension or further reinforcement. You may even decide to build an entire lesson around a spinner game. These mathematical spinner games are also an effective tool for encouraging parental involvement. They can be used during Family Math Nights, and they can be sent home on a regular basis for the whole family to enjoy.

HOW TO USE THE BOOK

Organization of Games

The games are grouped according to the NCTM standards for elementary school. This makes it easy for you to match games to the standards that you are working on. The first five standards (Problem Solving, Mathematical Communication, Reasoning, Mathematical Connections, and Estimation) are addressed in each of the spinner games. The remaining Standards, including Problem Solving and Mathematical Reasoning, serve as the topic headings under which the games are grouped:

- ⊗ Problem Solving and Mathematical Reasoning
- ⊗ Number Sense and Numeration
- ⊗ Whole-Number Operations
- ⊗ Geometry and Spatial Sense
- ⊗ Measurement
- ⊗ Probability
- ⊗ Fractions and Decimals

The spinner games are appropriate for grades 3 through 5. Each game is suitable for more than one grade level. The adaptability of the games makes them appropriate for a wide range of student abilities and thus they can be used in a heterogeneous class very effectively. You will want to decide for yourself which games are appropriate for your students.

Making the Spinners

Each game in this book is accompanied by a reproducible spinner template. You will also find that many of the number spinners can be purchased in school-supply stores. To make the spinners included here, just follow these simple directions:

- ⊗ Make a copy of the spinner and paste it to oaktag or cardboard for added durability.

⊛ Poke a hole though the center of the spinner using a brass fastener.

⊛ Then, open a paper clip into an S shape and slide the narrow end under the fastener. Squeeze the sides of the narrow end together to secure the paper clip.

⊛ Fold the ends of the fastener under the spinner leaving a little room so that the paper clip can spin with ease. You can either use the spinner as is, or tape one of the spinner arms from page 95 to the paper clip for added flair.

Game Components

Each game includes the following components:

Specification for the Number of Players
Each spinner game specifies the number of players that can play. Some games can be played individually, some in small groups, and some can be used as a whole-class activity.

A List of Necessary, Easy-to-Find Materials
Each spinner game lists the materials needed in order to play. For classroom management purposes, it is recommended that these materials be gathered prior to playing the game.

An Indication of the Math Skills the Game Reinforces
Each spinner game identifies the specific math skills it reinforces. Each skill and mathematical concept is outlined in the NCTM Standards.

Questions to Explore
These questions allow for additional enrichment experiences for each game. They are directed to the player in an effort to extend his thinking and emphasize reasoning processes. Each question gives students an opportunity to communicate their thinking and solutions to their classmates, families, or whomever they may be playing with. Hearing different problem-solving approaches helps students see that there are many possible strategies for solving the same problem.

Variations and Extensions
The Variations offer teachers specific strategies for adapting the game to different levels of ability.

The Extensions offer suggestions for extending the activity and skill beyond the game. Many of the extension activities are cross-curricular.

Problem Solving
and
Mathematical
Reasoning

① What's the Story?

Math Skills

⊗ Formulating problems from everyday and mathematical situations

⊗ Developing number and operation senses

⊗ Recognizing that several different problems can yield the same answer

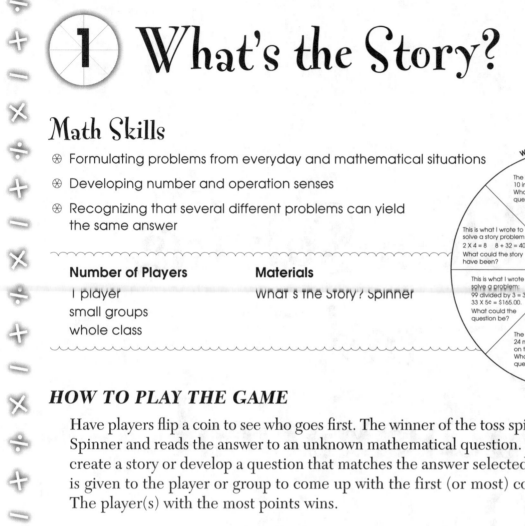

WHAT'S THE STORY? SPINNER

The answer is 10 inches. What could the question be?

The answer is 8. What could the question be?

This is what I wrote to solve a story problem:
2 X 4 = 8   8 + 32 = 40
What could the story have been?

The answer is $1/6$. What could the question be?

This is what I wrote to solve a problem:
99 divided by 3 = 33
33 X 5¢ = $165.00.
What could the question be?

Gummi bears cost 5¢ each. Soda costs 60¢. David has $1.50. What could the question be?

The answer is 24 miles per hour on the average. What could the question be?

Each cap costs $8.95. T-shirts are $12.30. The answer is 5. What could the question be?

Number of Players	Materials
1 player	What's the Story? Spinner
small groups	
whole class	

HOW TO PLAY THE GAME

Have players flip a coin to see who goes first. The winner of the toss spins the What's the Story? Spinner and reads the answer to an unknown mathematical question. The player(s) must then create a story or develop a question that matches the answer selected by the spinner. A point is given to the player or group to come up with the first (or most) correct story or question. The player(s) with the most points wins.

QUESTIONS TO EXPLORE

⊗ What strategies did you use to create the stories or develop questions?

VARIATIONS AND EXTENSIONS

1. Have students work together to brainstorm as many possible questions that can be developed from the same information. How are these questions similar? How are they different?

2. Have students create their own What's the Story? Spinners. Provide blank spinners and have students write mathematical answers in each space. Students can then exchange spinners and play the game.

25 SUPER-FUN MATH SPINNER GAMES
Scholastic Professional Books, 1997

Whatʼs the Story? Spinner

WHATʼS THE STORY? SPINNER

The answer is 10 inches. What could the question be?

The answer is 8. What could the question be?

This is what I wrote to solve a story problem:

2 X 4 = 8   8 + 32 = 40

What could the story have been?

The answer is $^1\!/_6$. What could the question be?

This is what I wrote to solve a problem:

99 divided by 3 = 33
33 X 5¢ = $165.00.

What could the question be?

Gummi bears cost 5¢ each. Soda costs 60¢. David has $1.50. What could the question be?

The answer is 24 miles per hour on the average. What could the question be?

Each cap costs $8.95. T-shirts are $12.30. The answer is 5. What could the question be?

(2) Coin Mysteries

Math Skills

⊗ Developing and applying strategies to solve problems

⊗ Using problem-solving approaches to investigate and understand mathematics

⊗ Using a variety of mental computation and estimation techniques

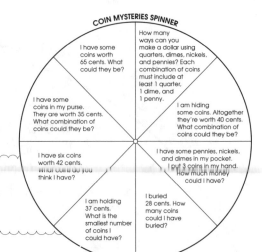

COIN MYSTERIES SPINNER

How many ways can you make a dollar using quarters, dimes, nickels, and pennies? Each combination of coins must include at least 1 quarter, 1 dime, and 1 penny.

I have some coins worth 65 cents. What could they be?

I have some coins in my purse. They are worth 35 cents. What combination of coins could they be?

I am hiding some coins. Altogether they're worth 40 cents. What combination of coins could they be?

I have some pennies, nickels, and dimes in my pocket. I put 3 coins in my hand. How much money could I have?

I have six coins worth 42 cents. What coins do you think I have?

I buried 28 cents. How many coins could I have buried?

I am holding 37 cents. What is the smallest number of coins I could have?

Number of Players	Materials
2–4 players in a group	Coin Mysteries Spinner number cube

HOW TO PLAY THE GAME

This game is played in cooperative groups. The goal of the game is to be the first group to come up with the correct answer(s) for each coin mystery. Each group selects a leader by rolling the number cube. The person with the largest number is the leader. The leader spins the Coin Mysteries Spinner and reads the coin mystery aloud. The groups have 4 minutes to try and come up with the correct response(s). The group that comes up with the correct answer, or the most correct answers when there is more than one possible outcome, gets a point. Once all the mysteries have been solved, play stops and the group with the most points wins.

QUESTIONS TO EXPLORE

⊗ What strategies did you use to play the game?

VARIATIONS AND EXTENSIONS

1. Have players create their own coin mysteries to explore.

25 SUPER-FUN MATH SPINNER GAMES
Scholastic Professional Books, 1997

 Coin Mysteries Spinner

COIN MYSTERIES SPINNER

How many ways can you make a dollar using quarters, dimes, nickels, and pennies? Each combination of coins must include at least 1 quarter, 1 dime, and 1 penny.

I have some coins worth 65 cents. What could they be?

I have some coins in my purse. They are worth 35 cents. What combination of coins could they be?

I am hiding some coins. Altogether they're worth 40 cents. What combination of coins could they be?

I have six coins worth 42 cents. What coins do you think I have?

I have some pennies, nickels, and dimes in my pocket. I put 3 coins in my hand. How much money could I have?

I am holding 37 cents. What is the smallest number of coins I could have?

I buried 28 cents. How many coins could I have buried?

③ Valuable Words

Math Skills

⊗ Using problem-solving strategies

⊗ Using a variety of mental computation skills

VALUABLE WORDS SPINNER

Most valuable 4-letter word
Least valuable 5-letter word
Word with a number of points that is a multiple of 5
Word with a number of points that is a multiple of 3
Most valuable 5-letter word
Word value between 50 and 70 points
Word value exactly 100 points
Least valuable 3-letter word
Most valuable 6-letter word
Word value less than 100
Least valuable 6-letter word
Most valuable 3-letter word

Number of Players	Materials
4–8 players	Letter Value Chart
whole class	Valuable Words Spinner
	recording sheet (optional)

HOW TO PLAY THE GAME

Distribute the Letter Value Chart and recording sheet (optional) to each player. Have the player with the "most valuable name" spin first to select the word category. Players must develop a word in that category. Each word's value is determined by adding up the number of points represented by the corresponding letters on the Letter Value Chart. For example, if the category were "Word value between 50 and 70 points," and a player formed the word "house," it would be worth 68 points. The first player to find a word within that category calls "Word," and if his word is appropriate (spelling and correct number of points calculated), he wins. Each player must keep track of these winning words, as no word may be used more than once. The winner is the player who reaches 10 points first.

QUESTIONS TO EXPLORE

⊗ What strategies did you use to try and think of a word for each category? Which strategies were more effective?

⊗ Were any of the categories easier (or harder) to find words for? If so, why?

VARIATIONS AND EXTENSIONS

1. Have players work in cooperative groups, rather than individually.

2. Players can try to develop as many words as possible for each of the selected categories, during a given time frame. The player or team with the most words, gets a point for that round.

3. Add a topic or theme to the game. For example, players may be asked to find "the most valuable 3-letter word that has to do with the theme of movement," rather than simply creating the "most valuable 3-letter word."

14

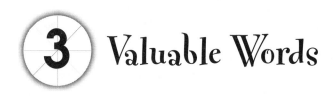 Valuable Words

LETTER VALUE CHART

A	B	C	D	E	F	G
1	2	3	4	5	6	7

H	I	J	K	L	M	N
8	9	10	11	12	13	14

O	P	Q	R	S	T	U
15	16	17	18	19	20	21

V	W	X	Y	Z
22	23	24	25	26

3 Valuable Words Spinner

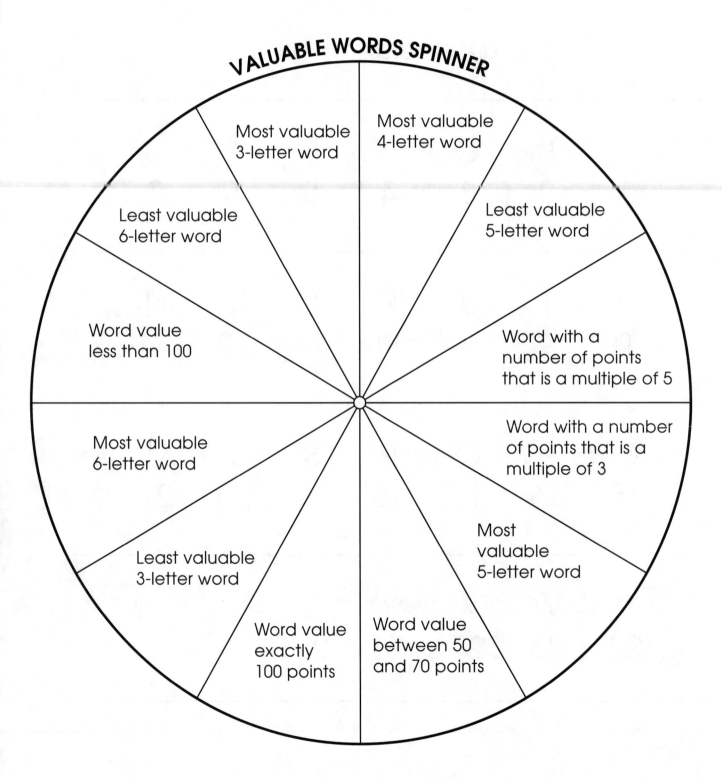

VALUABLE WORDS SPINNER

Most valuable 3-letter word

Most valuable 4-letter word

Least valuable 6-letter word

Least valuable 5-letter word

Word value less than 100

Word with a number of points that is a multiple of 5

Most valuable 6-letter word

Word with a number of points that is a multiple of 3

Least valuable 3-letter word

Most valuable 5-letter word

Word value exactly 100 points

Word value between 50 and 70 points

25 SUPER-FUN MATH SPINNER GAMES
Scholastic Professional Books, 1997

 Valuable Words Recording Sheet

Word value less than 100	Most valuable 6-letter word	Most valuable 4-letter word
Least valuable 6-letter word	Least valuable 3-letter word	Most valuable 3-letter word
Word value between 50 and 70 points	Word with a number of points that is a multiple of 3	Least valuable 5-letter word
Word with a number of points that is a multiple of 5	Most valuable 5-letter word	Word value exactly 100 points

Number Sense and Numeration

(4) What's in a Million?

Math Skills

⊗ Developing number sense

⊗ Interpreting the multiple uses of numbers in the real world

⊗ Using estimation

WHAT'S IN A MILLION? SPINNER

Having one million _____ could really be a problem.

I wish I had one million _____

If I had $1,000,000 to spend any way I wanted. I would _____

I could eat one million _____

I could never eat one million _____

I could hold one million _____

I would love to have one million _____

I could _____ one million times.

If I had one million _____, I would _____.

I could make one million _____

I could see one million _____

I could run one million _____

Number of Players	Materials
4–8 players	What's in a
whole class	Million? Spinner

HOW TO PLAY THE GAME

Players take turns being the leader. The leader spins and reads the incomplete sentence aloud for all the players to hear. The players must then think of a word or phrase to complete the sentence so that it makes sense. Encourage players to be as creative as possible in answering the questions. Have players share their responses after each round.

QUESTIONS TO EXPLORE

⊗ How did you figure out your answers?

VARIATIONS AND EXTENSIONS

1. To make this activity easier, change the number to 100 or 1000.

2. Have students use their responses as springboards for their creative writing by composing short stories that expand upon their answers.

3. Have students share each other's responses. Which ones came up most frequently?

25 SUPER-FUN MATH SPINNER GAMES
Scholastic Professional Books, 1997

4 What's in a Million? Spinner

WHAT'S IN A MILLION? SPINNER

I would love to have one million _____.

Having one million _____ could really be a problem.

I wish I had one million _____.

I could _____ one million times.

If I had $1,000,000 to spend any way I wanted, I would _____.

If I had one million _____, I would _____.

I could eat one million _____.

I could make one million _____.

I could never eat one million _____.

I could see one million _____.

I could hold one million _____.

I could run one million _____.

(5) Get the Largest Number

Math Skills

⊗ Understanding our numeration system by reading and comparing numbers

⊗ Developing place-value concepts and number sense

⊗ Exploring concepts of chance

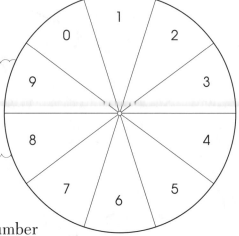

Number of Players	Materials	
2 players	Spinner with numbers 0–9 (p. 90)	
small group	paper	
whole class	scissors	pencil

HOW TO PLAY THE GAME

The goal of the game is to make the largest possible number with the digits selected by the spinner. Have each player create a game board by drawing four boxes and labeling them thousands, hundreds, tens, and ones from left to right.

A player spins the spinner and calls out the number selected. Each player must decide where to place that number on their game board—in the ones, tens, hundreds, or thousands place. Once players write a digit in a box, they cannot change it. Depending on the number of rounds you decide to play, the winner could either be the player who has created the largest number (if you only played one round) or the player whose numbers yield the largest sum after several rounds.

QUESTIONS TO EXPLORE

⊗ What strategies did you use to decide where to place the numbers as they came up? Play the game again to test the effectiveness of one strategy over another.

⊗ Work with a partner to create a list of all the possible combinations of numbers that could have been made with the digits that came up.

VARIATIONS AND EXTENSIONS

1. You could change the game by having students create numbers with additional or fewer number places.

2. You may change the object of the game so that players try to create the smallest number possible. You may even want to play with decimals.

3. Have players draw a "reject box" where they can discard one of the numbers selected by the spinner.

25 SUPER-FUN MATH SPINNER GAMES
Scholastic Professional Books, 1997

6 The Exchange Game

Math Skills

⊗ Developing an understanding of our numeration system by relating counting, grouping, and place-value concepts

⊗ Developing an understanding of regrouping in addition and subtraction using manipulatives

Number of Players	Materials
2–4 players	Exchange Game Board
	40 yellow markers
	40 green markers
	1 red marker
	Spinner with numbers 0–9 (p. 90)

HOW TO PLAY THE GAME

The goal of the game is to capture the red marker. Here, green markers represent 1s, yellow markers represent 10s and the red marker represents 100s. Players take turns spinning the spinner and taking the number of green markers indicated, which they then place in the green (or 1s) column on their game board. When a player finally collects 10 green markers, she exchanges them for 1 yellow marker. Play continues in this fashion until one player has collected 10 yellow markers (worth 100) and exchanges them for the red marker.

QUESTIONS TO EXPLORE:

⊗ Write an addition sentence to describe each move you made. For example, if the game board looks like the one shown here, and the spinner stops at 5, the player would write 27 + 5 = 32.

⊗ What did this game teach you about our number system?

EXCHANGE GAME BOARD

Red	Yellow	Green

VARIATIONS AND EXTENSIONS

1. Students can play the "Reverse Exchange Game". The goal of this game is to subtract green markers until the game board is empty of all markers. Begin the game with 1 red marker in the 100s place. Each player takes a turn spinning the spinner and removes the number of green markers indicated. For example, if a player spun 5, he would first have to exchange his red marker for 10 yellow markers and then would have to exchange 1 yellow marker for 10 green markers. Finally, he would remove 5 of the 10 green markers.

   The players keep exchanging yellow markers for green markers until all the markers are gone. The first player with an empty board wins.

2. You may change the game board by adding more columns to increase the place value. Here, blue markers represent 1,000s and orange markers represent 10,000s.

EXCHANGE GAME BOARD

Orange	Blue	Red	Yellow	Green

3. Players can modify the spinner so that it specifies the color marker to be removed in addition to the quantity.

25 SUPER-FUN MATH SPINNER GAMES
Scholastic Professional Books, 1997

EXCHANGE GAME BOARD

Red	Yellow	Green

(7) Boing!

Math Skills

⊗ Developing number sense

⊗ Using mental computation and estimation techniques

⊗ Using patterns and relationships to analyze mathematical situations

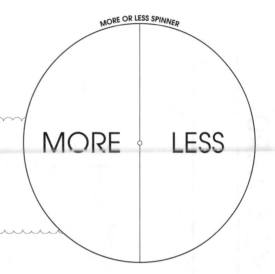

MORE OR LESS SPINNER

MORE | LESS

Number of Players	Materials
2–4 players	Hundred Chart
	More or Less Spinner
	Spinner with numbers 1–10 (p. 92)
	chips or markers

HOW TO PLAY THE GAME

The goal of the game is to get 4 markers in a row on the Hundred Chart horizontally, vertically, or diagonally. Each player is given a Hundred Chart and 12 markers, a different color for each player. Each player spins the number spinner; the player with the highest number goes first. She spins the number spinner again to select a number for that round. Then the player chooses a number—called the Boing!—on the Hundred Chart. Next, the player spins the More or Less Spinner. If the player gets "more," she must add the game number for that round to the Boing!; if she gets "less," then that game number must be subtracted from the Boing! Example: A player spins 6 as the game number for that round, then selects 30 as the Boing! Next, the player spins the More or Less Spinner. If it lands on "more," she must add 6 to 30 and place the marker on 36 on the Hundred Chart. If the spinner lands on "less," she would subtract 6 from 30, and place the marker on 24.

QUESTIONS TO EXPLORE

⊗ What patterns did you find that helped you get 4 markers in a row?

⊗ How did you decide on a Boing!?

VARIATIONS AND EXTENSIONS

1. Play with a smaller board (for example, numbers 1–50) or a larger board (numbers 1–200).

2. Create a spinner with the numbers 1–20 to make the addition and subtraction more difficult.

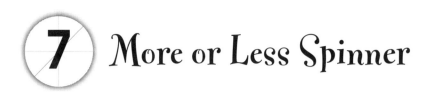

7 More or Less Spinner

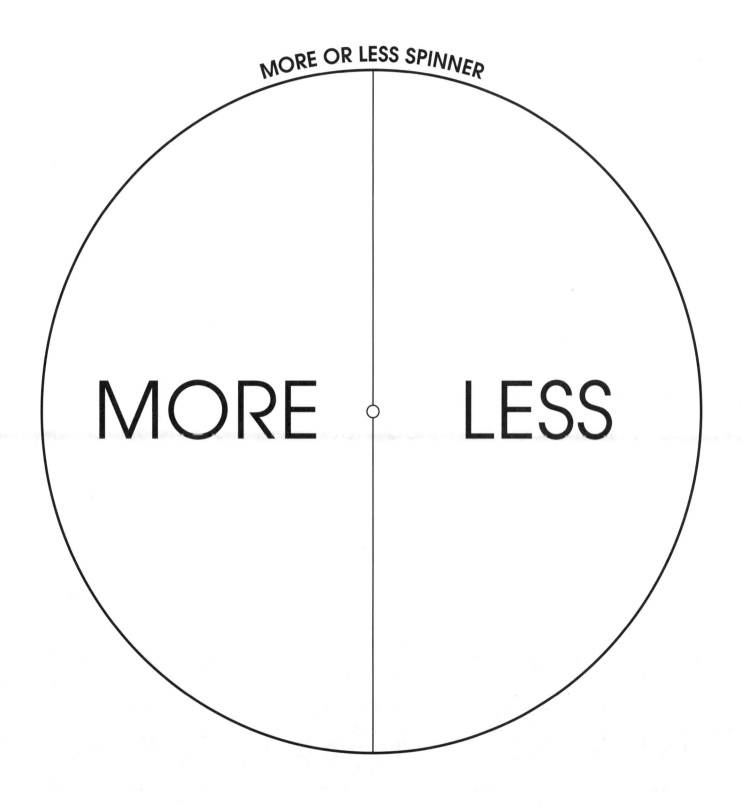

MORE OR LESS SPINNER

MORE · LESS

HUNDRED CHART

1	2	3	4	5	6	7	8	9	10
11	12	13	14	15	16	17	18	19	20
21	22	23	24	25	26	27	28	29	30
31	32	33	34	35	36	37	38	39	40
41	42	43	44	45	46	47	48	49	50
51	52	53	54	55	56	57	58	59	60
61	62	63	64	65	66	67	68	69	70
71	72	73	74	75	76	77	78	79	80
81	82	83	84	85	86	87	88	89	90
91	92	93	94	95	96	97	98	99	100

25 SUPER-FUN MATH SPINNER GAMES
Scholastic Professional Books, 1997

8 60 Wins

Math Skills

- ⊗ Understanding our numeration system by relating counting, grouping, and place-value concepts
- ⊗ Using patterns and relationships to analyze mathematical situations

60 WINS SPINNER

(Spinner divided into sections: Win 10, Lose 10, Win 1, Win 1, Win 10, Lose 1, Lose 10, Win 1, Win 10, Lose 1, Lose 10, Win 10)

Number of Players	Materials
2–4 players	60 kidney beans per player
whole class	60 Wins Spinner
	60 Wins Game Board

HOW TO PLAY THE GAME

The goal of the game is to be the first player to collect 60 beans and to fill each large pot on the game board with 10 beans. Each player is given a 60 Wins Game Board and a cup filled with 60 red kidney beans.

Each of the large pots on the game board holds 10 beans; each of the 9 smaller pots holds 1 bean. The first player spins the 60 Wins Spinner and adds or subtracts beans accordingly. For example, if the spinner stops at "Win 10," the player takes 10 beans from the cup and places them in a large pot on the game board. If the player spins "Win 1," she takes one bean and places it in a smaller pot. Once the player has collected 10 beans, she transfers them into a large pot. If the spinner stops at "Lose 10" or "Lose 1," the player must remove all 10 beans from a large pot or 1 bean from a smaller pot respectively. If a player has no beans, then there is nothing to remove. If the spinner asks the player to remove more beans than she has, she must remove all her beans, yet she does not owe any. The winner is the first player to fill each of the 6 large pots with 10 beans.

QUESTIONS TO EXPLORE

- ⊗ What does this game teach us about place value?
- ⊗ What is the least number of spins needed to win the game?

VARIATIONS AND EXTENSIONS

1. Ask the players to write number sentences to describe their moves.
2. You can change the game by using pennies and dimes as opposed to beans.

8 60 Wins Spinner

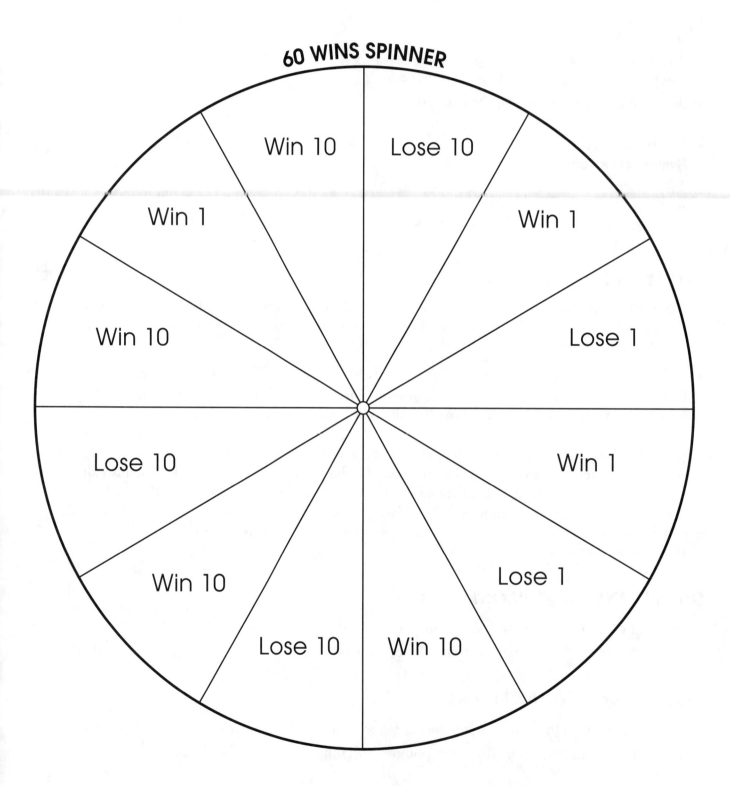

60 WINS SPINNER

Win 10

Lose 10

Win 1

Win 1

Win 10

Lose 1

Lose 10

Win 1

Win 10

Lose 1

Lose 10

Win 10

25 SUPER-FUN MATH SPINNER GAMES
Scholastic Professional Books, 1997

60 WINS GAME BOARD

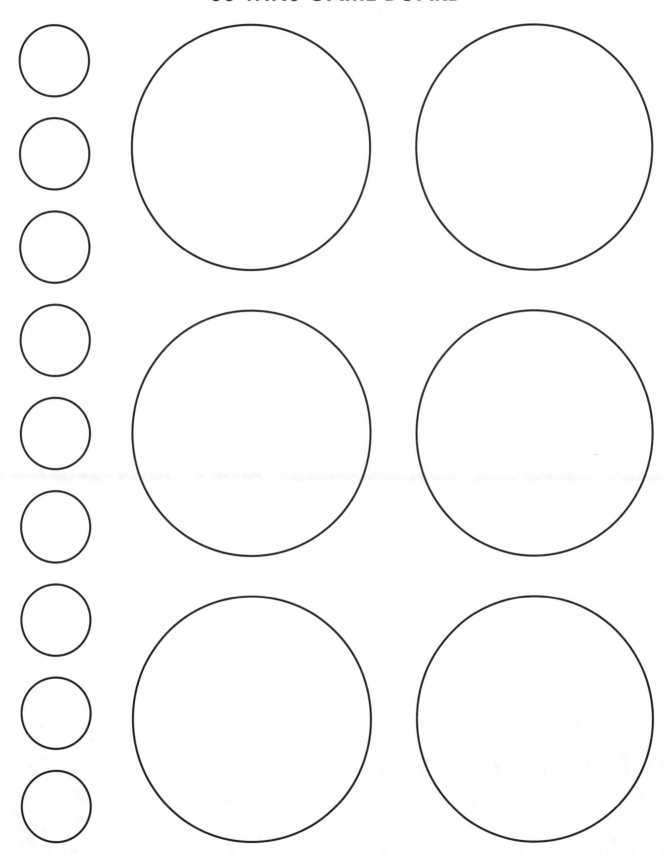

(9) Five in a Row

Math Skills

⊗ Developing number sense

⊗ Using patterns and relationships to analyze mathematical situations

⊗ Developing mental computation skills

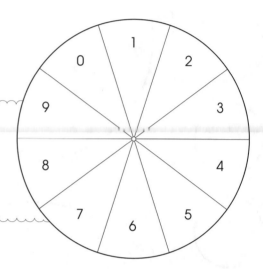

Number of Players	Materials
1 player	chips or markers (one color for each player)
2–4 players	
whole class	Spinner with numbers 0–9 (p. 90)
	Hundred Chart

HOW TO PLAY THE GAME

The goal of the game is to be the first player to have 5 counters in a row, either horizontally, vertically, or diagonally. Each player is given a copy of the Hundred Chart to use as a game board. Each player spins the number spinner twice, keeping track of the numbers selected. Then the player must perform a mathematical operation using the two numbers to create a new number that he or she covers with a chip. For example, if the spinner lands on 3 and 8, these two numbers could be combined in the following ways to make the following numbers:

> 3 tens and 8 ones = **38**
> 8 tens and 3 ones = **83**
> 3 + 8 = **11**
> 3 x 8 = **24**
> 8 - 3 = **5**

The player covers one of all the possible numbers that were created on the game board. The first player with 5 markers in a row in any direction is the winner.

QUESTIONS TO EXPLORE

⊗ What strategies did you use while playing the game?

VARIATIONS AND EXTENSIONS

1. To make the game go more quickly, have players cover all possible number combinations in one turn.

32

HUNDRED CHART

1	2	3	4	5	6	7	8	9	10
11	12	13	14	15	16	17	18	19	20
21	22	23	24	25	26	27	28	29	30
31	32	33	34	35	36	37	38	39	40
41	42	43	44	45	46	47	48	49	50
51	52	53	54	55	56	57	58	59	60
61	62	63	64	65	66	67	68	69	70
71	72	73	74	75	76	77	78	79	80
81	82	83	84	85	86	87	88	89	90
91	92	93	94	95	96	97	98	99	100

Whole-Number Operations

(10) What's the Problem?

Math Skills

- ⊗ Developing number and operation senses
- ⊗ Developing proficiency with basic facts and algorithms
- ⊗ Recognizing that a wide variety of problem structures can be represented by a single operation or a single number

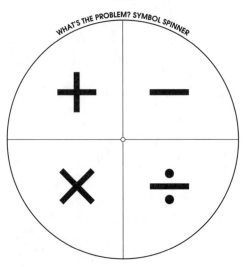

Number of Players	Materials
1 player	Answer Spinner
2 or more players	Symbol Spinner
	calculators

HOW TO PLAY THE GAME

The player spins the Answer Spinner for an answer to a number sentence and then spins the Symbol Spinner for an operation symbol. The player(s) must then create a number sentence using the indicated operation that yields the answer on the Answer Spinner. Players can check their work using a calculator.

> Example: A player spins the answer 70 and the minus symbol. The number sentence could be
> 100 - 30 = 70

The player or team with the greatest number of correct number sentences after 15 minutes wins.

QUESTIONS TO EXPLORE

- ⊗ What strategies did you use to create your number sentences?

VARIATIONS AND EXTENSIONS

1. Use a variety of number spinners to create a variety of number sentences. This game can be adapted for fractions, decimals, and positive and negative integers.

2. Take the game one step further by having students write word problems to illustrate each of their number sentences.

3. This game can be adapted for multi-operation number sentences by having each player spin the Symbol Spinner twice and use both operations in their number sentence.

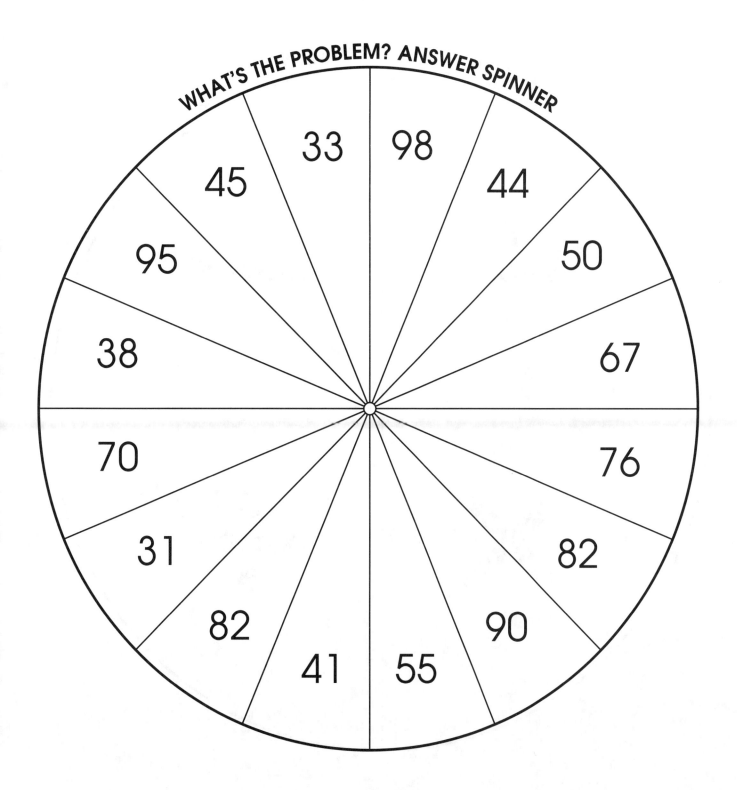

(10) What's the Problem? Symbol Spinner

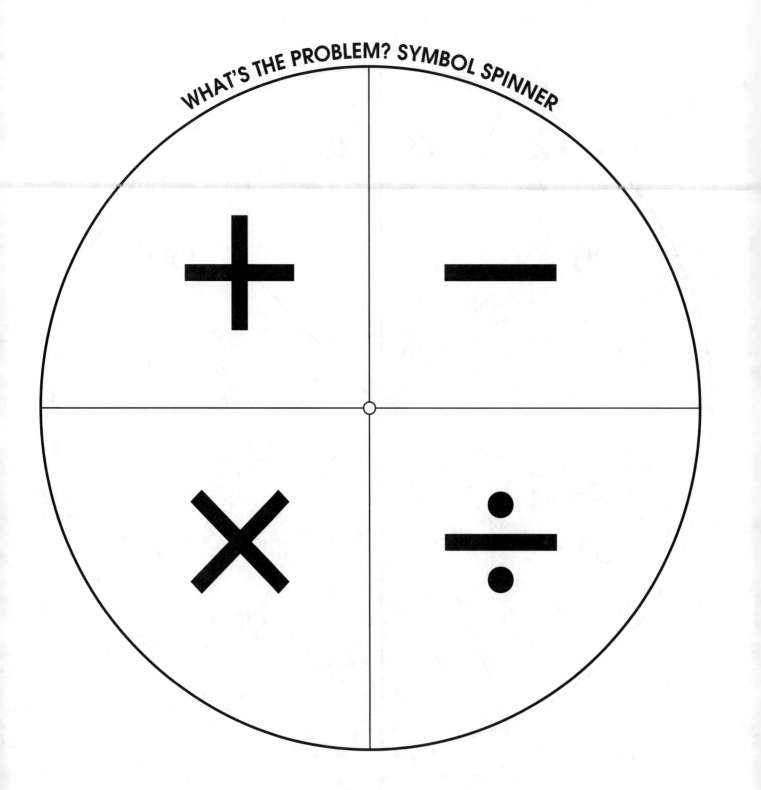

WHAT'S THE PROBLEM? SYMBOL SPINNER

25 SUPER-FUN MATH SPINNER GAMES
Scholastic Professional Books, 1997

(11) Destination Zero

Math Skills

⊗ Developing number sense

⊗ Using estimation and mental computation

⊗ Developing operation sense

⊗ Understanding our numeration system by reading and comparing numbers and place-value concepts

⊗ Exploring concepts of chance

Number of Players	Materials
2–4 players	Spinner with numbers 1–9 (p. 91)
whole class	paper and pencil

HOW TO PLAY THE GAME

The goal of the game is to be the first player to reach zero, or get closest to zero, without going below zero. Each player begins with 1000 points. The first player spins the spinner three times and makes a three-digit number. Then he subtracts that number from 1000. In subsequent turns, players can decide to create one-digit or two-digit numbers by spinning once or twice respectively. The game continues until one player reaches zero. If a player goes below zero, the game stops, and the winner is the one closest to yet above zero.

For example, if on the first spin, a player spun 4, the second spin 3, and the third spin 2, he or she could arrange the numerals as 432 and subtract that number from 1000 as on the right.

$$\begin{array}{r} 1000 \\ -432 \\ \hline 568 \end{array}$$

Since the difference is 568, there is a fair chance of getting at least one number that is less than 5. Therefore, on the next spin, the player may decide to spin three times. If the spinner stops at 4, 2, and 9, and he or she forms the number 492, 492 would be subtracted from 568 to get 76.

$$\begin{array}{r} 568 \\ -492 \\ \hline 76 \end{array}$$

On the next spin, the player would only spin twice, since 76 is a two-digit number. If the spinner stops at 6 and 9, the player would decide to form the number 69, since 96 is greater than 76. Then he or she would subtract 69 from 76 to get 7.

$$\begin{array}{r} 76 \\ -69 \\ \hline 7 \end{array}$$

While some players might decide to hold with a number as low as 7, others might decide to chance it and spin again. If the player spun a 3, he or she would subtract 3 from 7 to get 4.

$$\begin{array}{r} 7 \\ -3 \\ \hline 4 \end{array}$$

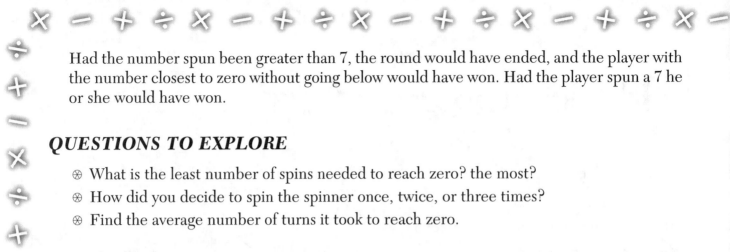

Had the number spun been greater than 7, the round would have ended, and the player with the number closest to zero without going below would have won. Had the player spun a 7 he or she would have won.

QUESTIONS TO EXPLORE

⊗ What is the least number of spins needed to reach zero? the most?

⊗ How did you decide to spin the spinner once, twice, or three times?

⊗ Find the average number of turns it took to reach zero.

VARIATIONS AND EXTENSIONS

1. Play the game "Destination 1000." The goal of the game is to be the first player to reach 1000 without going over. The players begin with zero and spin the spinner to make a three-digit number to add to zero. After their first turn, players can decide to spin once, twice, or three times to form one-digit, two-digit, or three-digit numbers. The player whose sum is the closest to, but not greater than, 1000 is the winner.

   A sample game may look like this:

   1st turn: Danielle spun the spinner three times.
   She got 6, 8, and 2.
   She formed 862.

   2nd turn: She spun the spinner twice.
   She got 7 and 6.
   She formed 76.
   862 + 76 = 938

   3rd turn: She spun the spinner twice.
   She got 5 and 2.
   She formed 52.
   938 + 52 = 990

   4th turn: She spun the spinner once.
   She got 6.
   990 + 6 = 996
   She stopped.

2. You can also have students play the game with fractions and decimals.

3. To make the game easier, use 100 instead of 1,000 as your starting point or your destination.

4. To practice multiplication, have the players multiply the two numbers and subtract the product from 1,000 or 100 to reach zero.

(12) Cross It Out!

Math Skills

⊗ Developing number sense

⊗ Using estimation and mental computation

⊗ Developing operation sense

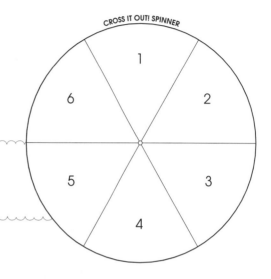

Number of Players	**Materials**
2–4 players	Cross It Out! Spinner
whole class	

HOW TO PLAY THE GAME

The goal of the game is to be the first player to cross out all the numbers on a list. Each player writes the numbers 1–12 on a piece of paper. The first player spins the spinner twice and adds the two numbers. The player then has the option of crossing that number or its addends from the list. For example, if the player spins a 5 and a 6, he can choose to cross out 11, or 5 and 6, or 7 and 4, or 8 and 3, or 9 and 2, or 10 and 1, or 1, 2, and 8. The first player to cross out all 12 numbers is the winner.

QUESTIONS TO EXPLORE

⊗ What strategies did you use to play the game?

VARIATIONS AND EXTENSIONS

1. Use a different spinner, for example one with numbers 1–10. This time, have players write the numbers 1–30 on a piece of paper and cross them out.

2. Ask the players to make up their own variation of this game.

(12) Cross It Out! Spinner

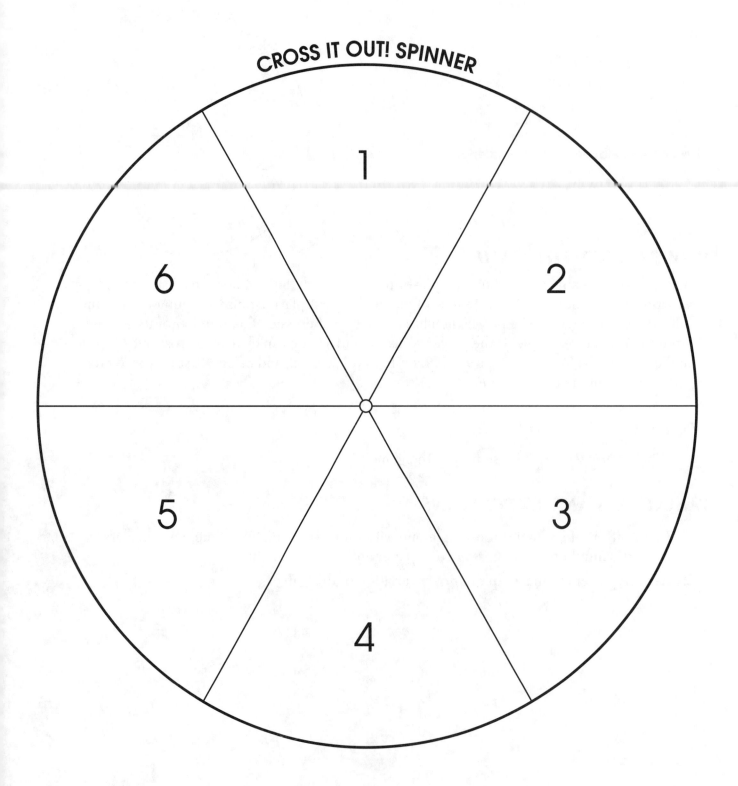

CROSS IT OUT! SPINNER

1

2

3

4

5

6

25 SUPER-FUN MATH SPINNER GAMES
Scholastic Professional Books, 1997

13 Five Spin

Math Skills

⊗ Developing number sense

⊗ Using mental computation and estimation techniques

⊗ Developing operation sense

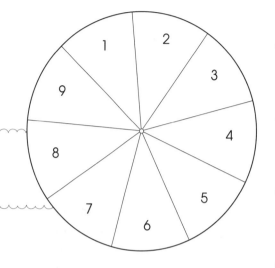

Number of Players	Materials
2–4 players whole class	Spinner with numbers 1–9 (p. 91)

HOW TO PLAY THE GAME

To start off, one player spins the spinner four times and calls out the numbers for all the players to record. Then he spins the spinner again, to identify the key number. The object of the game is for players to combine the first 4 numbers in some fashion to arrive at the key number. Players can use any or all operations as many times as necessary.

For example, if a player spun the following numbers:

First four numbers: 5 2 3 8

Key number: 4

She might perform the following operations to arrive at the key number—4.

$5 \times 2 = 10$ $10 - 3 = 7$ $7 + 2 = 9$ $9 - 5 = 4$

The first player to combine the numbers and arrive at the key number without making any computational errors wins.

QUESTIONS TO EXPLORE

⊗ What strategies did you use to try and get the key number?

⊗ Which operation did you use most often? Did you do the computations in your head?

VARIATIONS AND EXTENSIONS

1. You could change the game by creating a spinner with the numbers 1–20, decimals, a combination of negative and positive integers, or Roman Numerals.

2. You may also have players spin more than 5 times.

3. Students can create word problems to illustrate the sequence of their number sentences.

(14) Four Spinner Bingo

Math Skills

⊗ Modeling, explaining and developing reasonable proficiency with basic facts and algorithms

⊗ Reinforcing multiplication skills

⊗ Using mental computation

⊗ Developing operation sense by recognizing numerical patterns

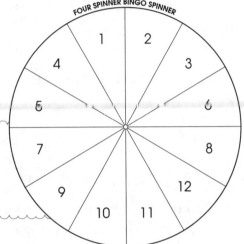

FOUR SPINNER BINGO SPINNER

Number of Players	Materials
2–4 players	Four Spinner Bingo Spinner
	1 Multiplication Grid per player
	chips or markers

HOW TO PLAY THE GAME

The goal of the game is to be the first player to fill a row of numbers vertically or horizontally on the Multiplication Grid. Players will need a new grid for each new game. Each player spins the spinner twice, multiplies the two numbers, and covers the product on the Multiplication Grid wherever it appears. If, for example, a player spun the numbers 2 and 4 and multiplied them to get 8, she could cover 8 where it is a product of 2 and 4 or 8 and 1. The winner is the first player to fill an entire row either horizontally or vertically.

QUESTIONS TO EXPLORE

⊗ Do you notice any patterns on your Multiplication Grid? Did you notice, for example, that all multiples of 5 end in 5 or 0, and that all multiples of 11 increase by one digit in the 1s place?

VARIATIONS AND EXTENSIONS

1. To make the game easier, use a simpler Multiplication Grid and a spinner with the numbers 1–6.

2. This game can be adapted using addition, subtraction, or division facts.

3. Have each player pick a number from 1 through 12 and write down all the multiples of that number up to 144. The players then find all the places where that number and its multiples appear and color those squares. Have students compare the patterns that the different numbers make.

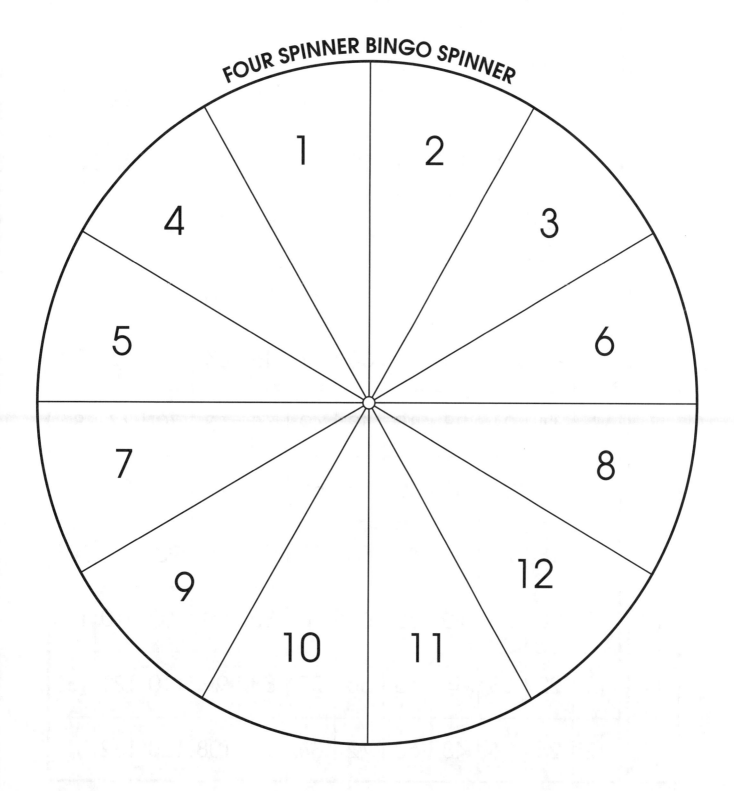

FOUR SPINNER BINGO SPINNER

1 2 3 4 5 6 7 8 9 10 11 12

MULTIPLICATION GRID

X	1	2	3	4	5	6	7	8	9	10	11	12
1	1	2	3	4	5	6	7	8	9	10	11	12
2	2	4	6	8	10	12	14	16	18	20	22	24
3	3	6	9	12	15	18	21	24	27	30	33	36
4	4	8	12	16	20	24	28	32	36	40	44	48
5	5	10	15	20	25	30	35	40	45	50	55	60
6	6	12	18	24	30	36	42	48	54	60	66	72
7	7	14	21	28	35	42	49	56	63	70	77	84
8	8	16	24	32	40	48	56	64	72	80	88	96
9	9	18	27	36	45	54	63	72	81	90	99	108
10	10	20	30	40	50	60	70	80	90	100	110	120
11	11	22	33	44	55	66	77	88	99	110	121	132
12	12	24	36	48	60	72	84	96	108	120	132	144

25 SUPER-FUN MATH SPINNER GAMES
Scholastic Professional Books, 1997

Divingo

Math Skills

⊗ Developing number sense

⊗ Using estimation and mental computation

⊗ Developing operation sense

⊗ Reinforcing basic division facts

⊗ Exploring concepts of chance

Number of Players	**Materials**
any number of players	Spinner with numbers 0–9 (p. 90)
	1 Divingo Game Board per player

HOW TO PLAY THE GAME:

The goal of the game is to be the first player to complete three division problems horizontally, vertically, or diagonally on the Divingo Game Board. Players can work independently or cooperatively. Use the blank Divingo Game Board on page 50 to create as many different boards as possible by changing the location of the problems. The leader spins the spinner once and calls out the selected numeral. Each player chooses a square within a division problem and places the selected numeral in that square. Once placed, a numeral cannot be moved, but if the spinner lands on the same number again, it can be played. Only problems with remainders of zero are allowed.

Here is an example. Say the following numbers were called:

1, 8, 0, 9, 4, 7, 3, 2, 3, 6, 9, 6, and 1. They could be placed on the board in the following way to win the game:

DIVINGO GAME BOARD

9	3	4
10 9 0	2 ☐ 6	8 3 2
☐	6	☐
1 ☐ 1	3 1 8	4 ☐ ☐
☐	☐	☐
5 ☐ ☐	6 ☐ ☐	7 7 ☐

QUESTIONS TO EXPLORE

⊗ What strategies did you use to play the game?

VARIATIONS AND EXTENSIONS

1. Adapt the Divingo Game Board for more difficult division problems involving 3-digit numbers.

2. Players can create a "reject box" where they can dispose of numbers they do not want to use.

DIVINGO GAME BOARD

10	2	8
1	3	4
5	6	7

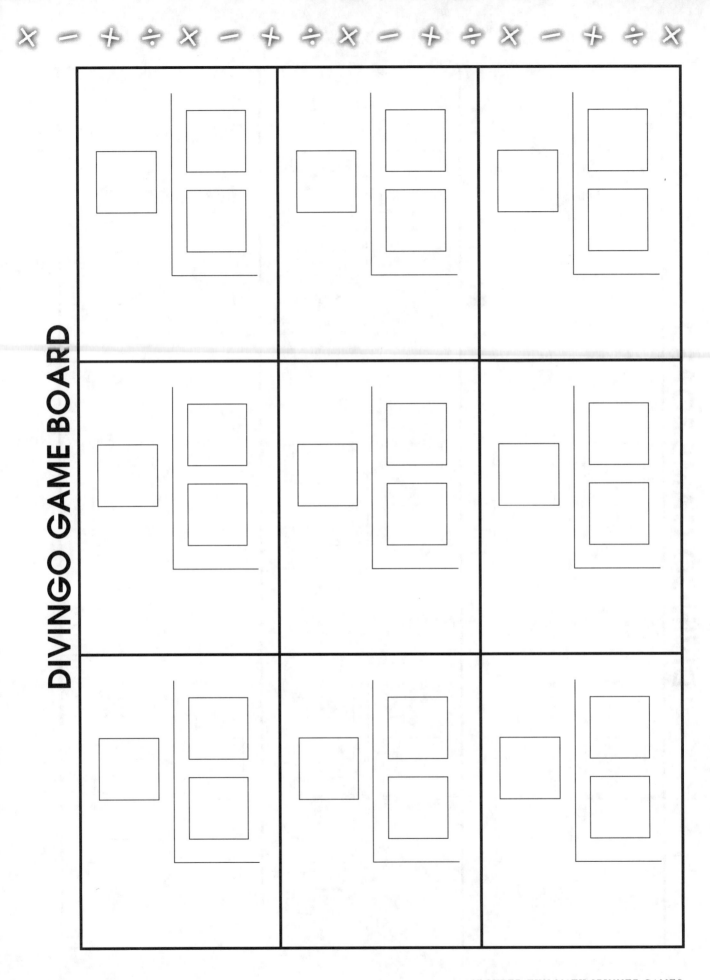

DIVINGO GAME BOARD

Geometry
and
Spatial Sense

(16) Coordinate Tic-Tac-Toe

Math Skills

⊗ Understanding coordinates and graphing points on a grid

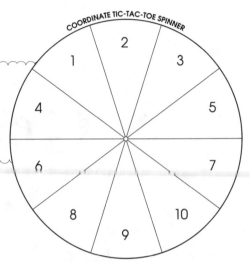

COORDINATE TIC-TAC-TOE SPINNER

Number of Players	Materials
2 players or 2 teams	Coordinate Tic-Tac-Toe Spinner
	1 sheet of 1/4-inch graph paper per student

HOW TO PLAY THE GAME

The goal of the game is to get four Xs or four Os in a row along the intersections of the graph paper game board. Once players have decided which letter they will be, the first player spins the spinner once to identify a number. He then selects any other number to form an ordered pair—the two numbers that name an intersection, or a point on the graph. The ordered pair is always written in parentheses. Once the player has named his intersection, he marks it with his letter.

For example, if a player spins 5 and then picks 9, he would place an X or an O at the intersection of (5, 9). Players take turns naming and marking points of intersection. The first player with four Xs or Os in a row is the winner.

QUESTIONS TO EXPLORE

⊗ What strategies did you use to choose the second number? What influenced your decisions?

VARIATIONS AND EXTENSIONS

1. Play with four players and assign each a different symbol.

25 SUPER-FUN MATH SPINNER GAMES
Scholastic Professional Books, 1997

16 Coordinate Tic-Tac-Toe Spinner

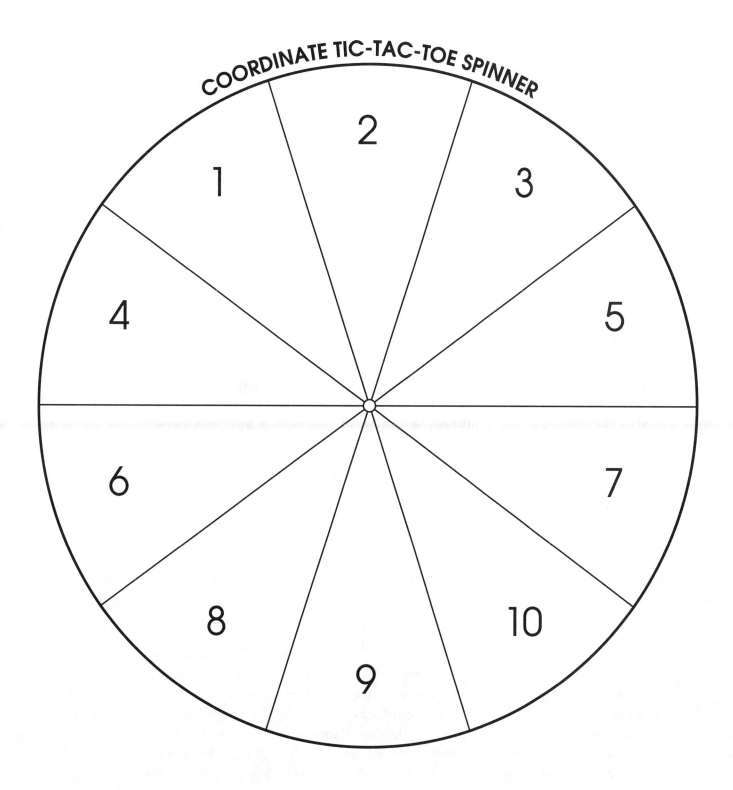

COORDINATE TIC-TAC-TOE SPINNER

1 2 3 4 5 6 7 8 9 10

(17) Pentamino Spin

Math Skills

⊗ Developing spatial sense

⊗ Investigating and predicting the results of combining and changing shapes

⊗ Describing, drawing, and classifying shapes

⊗ Exploring geometric transformations and congruence

PENTAMINO SPINNER

Number of Players	Materials
2 players	1 sheet of 1-inch graph paper per student
	Pentamino Spinner
	crayons or colored pencils
	scissors

Spinner sections: Color 2, Color 1, Color 3, Color 4, Color 1, Color 1, SKIP A TURN, Color 2

HOW TO PLAY THE GAME

The goal of the game is to arrange five squares to make as many different pentamino shapes as possible using the graph paper. The player with the most pentamino shapes is the winner. In coloring the five squares to make pentaminoes, the rule is that each of the squares must share a full side with at least one other square.

This is a pentamino—all 5 squares share one full side with another square.

These are not pentaminoes—some squares share full sides, but not all 5.

In this game, each pentamino shape made must be different, and not congruent. Pentamino shapes that are congruent will be considered the same. If one pentamino shape can be flipped or rotated so that it fits exactly on another, the two shapes are congruent and thus, the same.

different   not different, but congruent

Here's how to play: The first player spins and colors the number of squares indicated to start a pentamino. The second player then spins and tries to build upon the first player's pentamino by adding the number of squares indicated. However, if the first player spun "Color 4 Squares," the only way the second player could add to the pentamino was if he spun "Color 1 Square" as pentaminoes are composed of 5 squares. If the spinner had asked the second

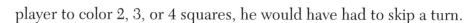

player to color 2, 3, or 4 squares, he would have had to skip a turn.

The player to place the fifth square and form the pentamino gets to claim that shape. Players continue to color and collect shapes until all 12 pentamino shapes have been made. The player who claimed the most shapes wins.

QUESTIONS TO EXPLORE

⊗ How did you go about trying to arrange the squares into different pentamino shapes?

⊗ Are all the perimeters of the various pentamino shapes the same? If not, which has the largest perimeter? Which has the smallest? Do all the pentaminoes have the same area? What conclusions can you make regarding the perimeters of these figures in relation to the area?

⊗ Are any of the pentaminoes quadrilaterals? pentagons? hexagons? octagons? decagons?

VARIATIONS AND EXTENSIONS

1. Have the groups classify the pentamino shapes into those that can be folded into a box and those that cannot, and those that are symmetrical and those that aren't.

2. Play the game with varying sized shapes. For example: Find all the ways to arrange 3 squares, 4 squares, or 6 squares.

3. Have players cut out all 12 pentamino shapes and arrange them into a rectangle. What is the perimeter of the rectangle? What is the area?

4. Have the different groups match congruent pentamino shapes.

The 12 Pentaminoes

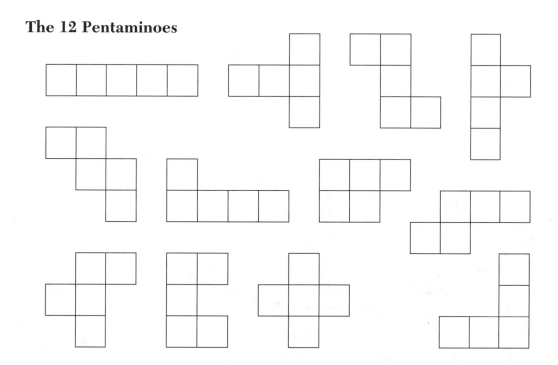

(17) Pentamino Spinner

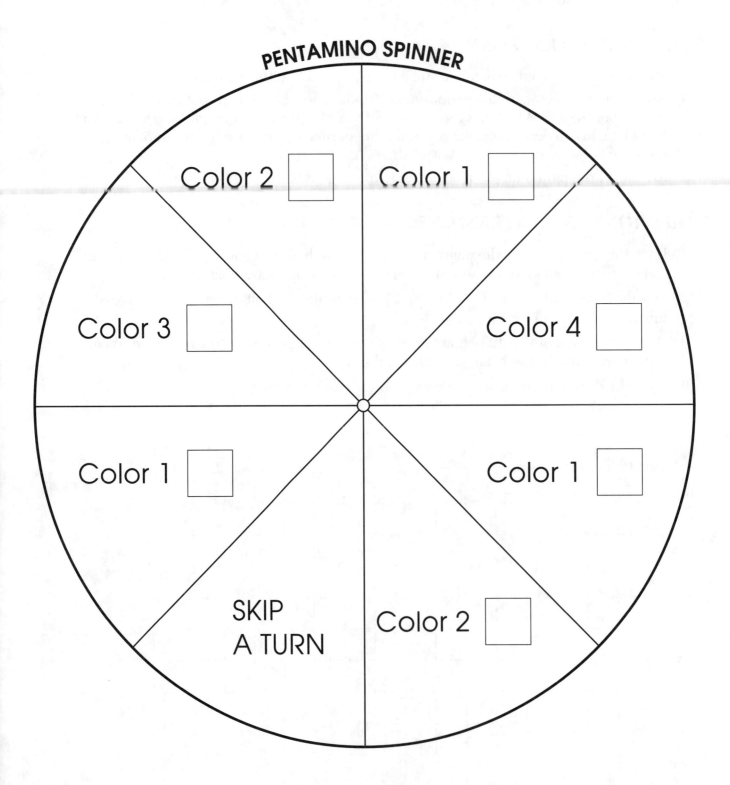

PENTAMINO SPINNER

Color 2 ☐   Color 1 ☐

Color 3 ☐   Color 4 ☐

Color 1 ☐   Color 1 ☐

SKIP
A TURN   Color 2 ☐

25 SUPER-FUN MATH SPINNER GAMES
Scholastic Professional Books, 1997

(18) Patchwork Quilt Spin

Math Skills

⊗ Identifying and describing geometric shapes

⊗ Recognizing lines of symmetry

PATCHWORK QUILT SPINNER

| 1 | 2 |
| 3 | 4 |

Number of Players	Materials
2–4 players	Patchwork Quilt Spinner
	Patchwork Quilt Game Board
	Patchwork Quilt Cut Outs (p. 61)
	colored counters
	glue
	construction paper

HOW TO PLAY THE GAME

The goal of the game is to be the first player to move around the Patchwork Quilt Game Board. As players move around the board, they collect geometric shapes to make their own patchwork quilt. Make several copies of the Patchwork Quilt Cut Outs, cut them apart, and place them in a container next to the board. Each player spins the Patchwork Quilt Spinner and moves his playing piece the number of spaces selected. The player then takes the geometric shape indicated on the space where he landed from the container. Landing on a "Free Pick" space entitles the player to pick the shape of his choice. Landing on a "Lose Your Turn" space prevents the player from picking a shape. The first player to reach "Home" wins.

At the completion of the game, players make their own patchwork quilts using the shapes they collected as they went around the board. Encourage players to create quilts that have lines of symmetry.

QUESTIONS TO EXPLORE

⊗ While some patchwork quilt designs are "crazy" and based on random shapes, most are carefully planned and based on geometric relationships that are symmetrical. Is your patchwork quilt "crazy" or symmetrical? Explain why. If you wanted to make sure that your quilt was symmetrical, how would that influence your selection of geometric shapes when you landed on the "Free Pick" space?

VARIATIONS AND EXTENSIONS

1. Patchwork quilt patterns provide a wonderful springboard for developing mathematical concepts. Have the children design a patchwork quilt pattern based on one shape, two shapes, and so on. Ask them to describe each other's patterns using mathematical language.

2. Use patchwork quilt patterns to develop fraction concepts.

    Example: What fraction of the whole pattern is the triangular piece? the square piece? the rectangular piece?

3. Use patchwork quilt patterns to develop measurement concepts.

    Example: What is the area of each square if the sides of the outer square measure 5 inches each?

    (Hint: All of the triangles are equilateral. Once you determine the length of their sides, you should be able to find the area of each square.)

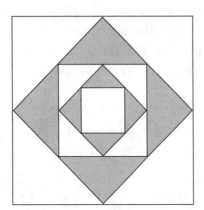

18 Patchwork Quilt Spinner

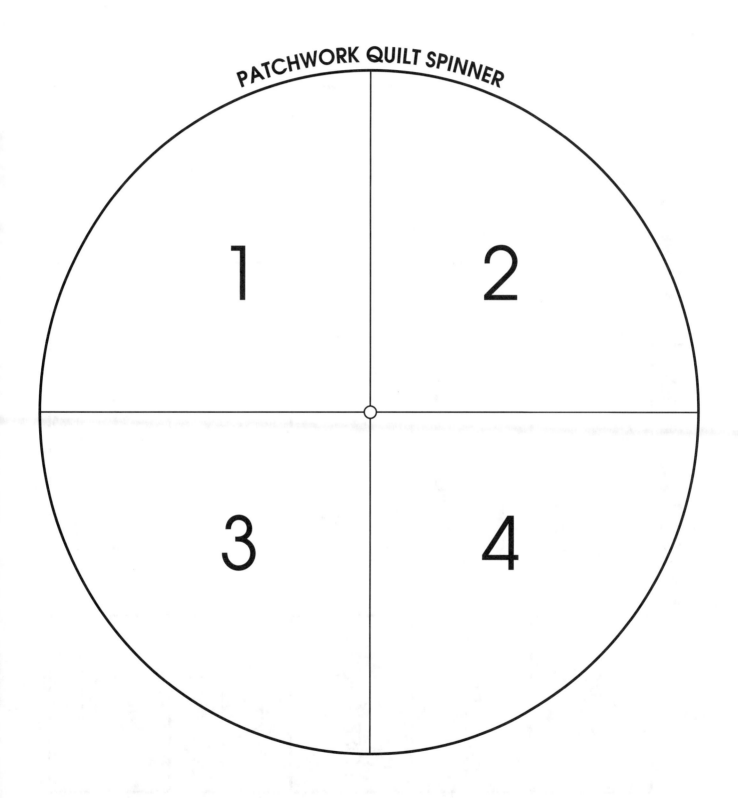

PATCHWORK QUILT SPINNER

1   2

3   4

PATCHWORK QUILT GAME BOARD

triangle	rectangle	circle	square	START
hexagon	oval	rhombus	parallelogram	FREE PICK
FREE PICK	triangle	rectangle	circle	LOSE A TURN
pentagon	octagon	LOSE A TURN	square	parallelogram
HOME	FREE PICK	square	oval	triangle

25 SUPER-FUN MATH SPINNER GAMES
Scholastic Professional Books, 1997

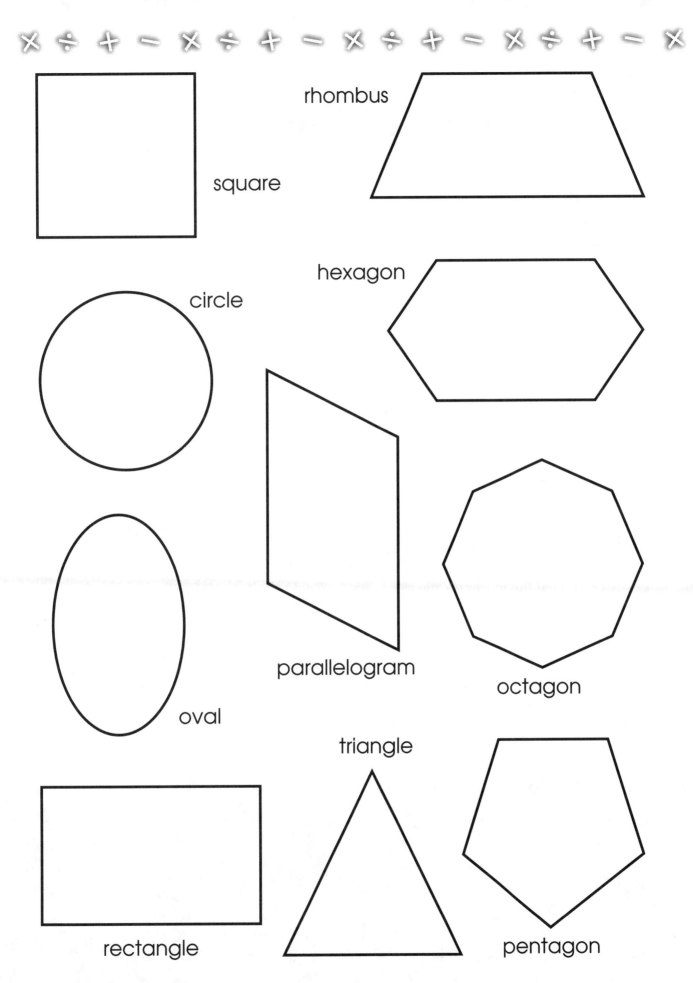

square

rhombus

circle

hexagon

oval

parallelogram

octagon

triangle

rectangle

pentagon

(19) Toothpick Mania

Math Skills

⊗ Developing spatial sense

⊗ Recognizing and appreciating geometry

⊗ Describing, modeling, and classifying shapes

⊗ Investigating and predicting the results of combining and changing shapes

⊗ Using a trial-and-error strategy

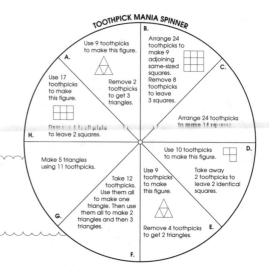

Number of Players	Materials
1–2 Players	Toothpick Mania Spinner 30 Toothpicks per player

HOW TO PLAY THE GAME

Players take turns spinning the spinner and trying to solve the toothpick puzzle it lands on. If a player is not able to complete the spinner challenge successfully within a certain time frame, he must pass and the next player spins. Likewise, if the spinner stops at a challenge that has already been completed successfully, that player must skip a turn and the next player goes. Once all the toothpick puzzles have been solved, the player with the greatest number of successfully completed toothpick challenges wins.

QUESTIONS TO EXPLORE

⊗ What strategies did you use to solve these toothpick puzzles? Which ones were easier and which were harder?

⊗ If you made one triangle with 12 toothpicks, what different types of triangles would they be? How many different types can you make?

VARIATIONS AND EXTENSIONS

1. Invite players to create their own toothpick puzzles.

Answers to Toothpick Puzzles

A.

B.

C.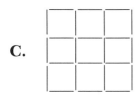

D.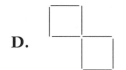

E.

F.

2 triangles

3 triangles

G.

H.

19 Toothpick Mania Spinner

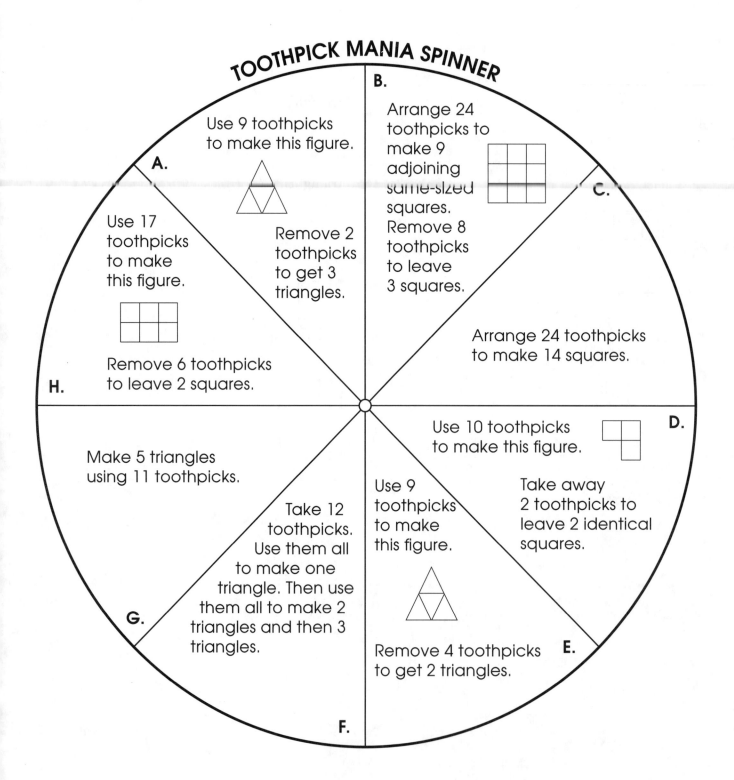

TOOTHPICK MANIA SPINNER

A. Use 9 toothpicks to make this figure.

Remove 2 toothpicks to get 3 triangles.

B. Arrange 24 toothpicks to make 9 adjoining same-sized squares. Remove 8 toothpicks to leave 3 squares.

C. Arrange 24 toothpicks to make 14 squares.

D. Use 10 toothpicks to make this figure.

Take away 2 toothpicks to leave 2 identical squares.

E. Remove 4 toothpicks to get 2 triangles.

Use 9 toothpicks to make this figure.

F. Take 12 toothpicks. Use them all to make one triangle. Then use them all to make 2 triangles and then 3 triangles.

G. Make 5 triangles using 11 toothpicks.

H. Remove 6 toothpicks to leave 2 squares.

Use 17 toothpicks to make this figure.

25 SUPER-FUN MATH SPINNER GAMES
Scholastic Professional Books, 1997

Measurement

20 Guess and Measure

Math Skills

⊗ Estimating and measuring length

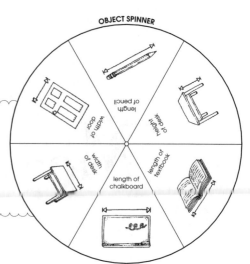

OBJECT SPINNER

Number of Players	Materials
teams of 2	Object Spinner
	Units of Measure Spinner
	Guess and Measure Recording Sheet
	rulers with inches, mm, and cm units

HOW TO PLAY THE GAME

Players flip a coin to pick a leader. The leader spins the Object Spinner and each player writes the name of the object in the "Round One Object" row of the Guess and Measure Recording Sheet. Next, the leader spins the Units of Measure Spinner and players record the selected unit for that round in the Unit of Measure Column. If the spinner stops at "Your Choice", teams select their own unit of measure.

Players record their estimates of the length or height of the object using the selected unit of measure. Once everyone has written down their estimate, the leader measures the object. Players then record the exact measurement on their Recording Sheets and then find the difference between that number and their estimate. If the leader spins the same object and the same unit of measure in more than one round (i.e., inches and width of textbook), he must pass the spinners on to the next player who then becomes the leader.

After 6 rounds, have players find the total difference between their estimates and the actual measurements. The player(s) whose estimates were closest to the actual measurements wins.

QUESTIONS TO EXPLORE

⊗ Did your estimates improve as you played the game?

⊗ Was there one unit of measure you were better able to estimate than another (i.e., inches vs. centimeters)?

VARIATIONS AND EXTENSIONS

1. Have students create their own Guess and Measure Spinners. They can select different objects to measure as well as different ways of measuring them—lengths of yarn, length of a pencil, height of a teddy bear, etc.

25 SUPER-FUN MATH SPINNER GAMES
Scholastic Professional Books, 1997

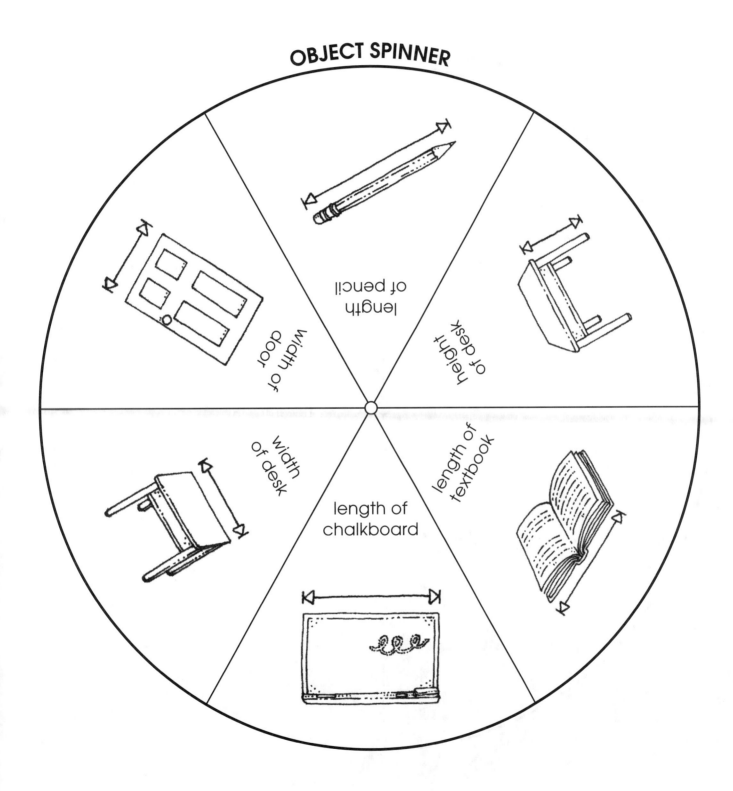

OBJECT SPINNER

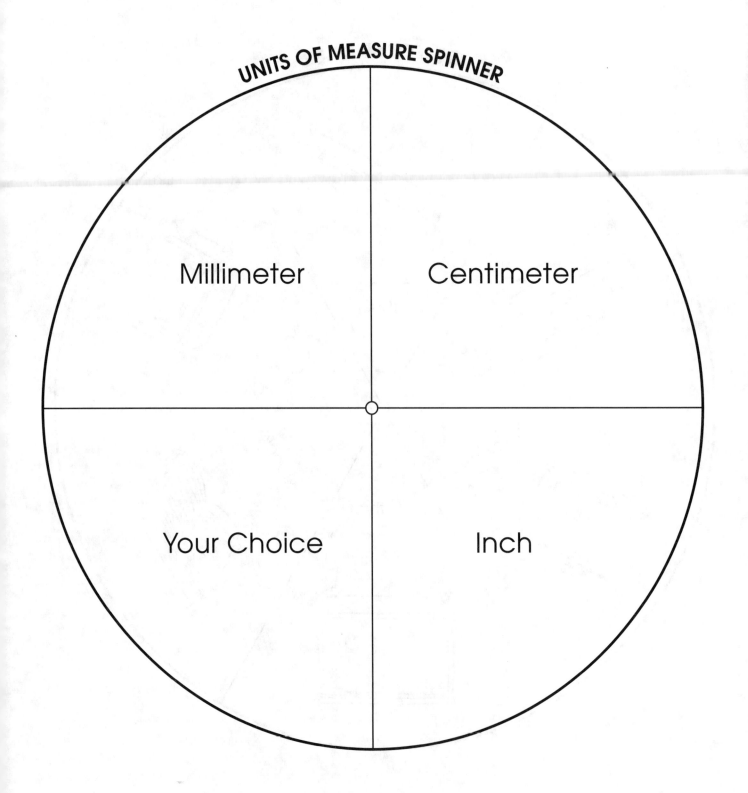

20 Units of Measure Spinner

UNITS OF MEASURE SPINNER

Millimeter

Centimeter

Your Choice

Inch

25 SUPER-FUN MATH SPINNER GAMES
Scholastic Professional Books, 1997

GUESS AND MEASURE RECORDING SHEET

Round	Object	Unit of Measure	Estimate	Actual Measurement	Difference
1					
2					
3					
4					
5					
6					

Total Difference

Probability

㉑ Spinner Sum Predictions

Math Skills

⊗ Exploring concepts of chance

⊗ Solving problems that involve collecting and analyzing data

SPINNER SUM PREDICTIONS SPINNER

1	2
3	4

Number of Players	**Materials**
teams of 2	Spinner Sum Predictions Spinner
	1 sheet of 1/4-inch graph paper

HOW TO PLAY THE GAME

In this probability experiment, teams try to predict how many times they will get the same answer when adding numbers from the Spinner Sum Predictions Spinner. Have players create recording sheets by labeling 10 columns on the graph paper with the numbers 1–10, and labeling 30 rows with the numbers 1–30. Here, the numbers 1–10 represent the range of possible sums and the numbers 1–30 represent the number of times each team will spin and record its answer. Both team members spin once, add their numbers, and record the sum on the graph paper.

Before beginning, have players predict and record which sum they think will appear most often. After 30 tries, have teams count the total number of times they formed each sum. The team(s) whose answer is closest to its prediction wins.

QUESTIONS TO EXPLORE

⊗ Were the results of this experiment the same as your predictions? Why do you think?

⊗ Do you think that all the teams will have the same results? Why or why not?

VARIATIONS AND EXTENSIONS

1. As students think about their answers to question 2 above, engage them in a conversation about the possible number combinations for each sum. With your help students will realize that sums of 2, 3, 7, and 8 have the least probability (i.e., least possible combinations), and the sums of 4, 5, and 6 have the greatest probability (i.e., most possible combinations).

Sum of 2	1+1			Sum of 5	2+3	4+1	Sum of 7	3+4
Sum of 3	2+1			Sum of 6	2+4	3+3	Sum of 8	4+4
Sum of 4	2+2	3+1						

2. Have students play Spinner Product Predictions. In this game students multiply the 2 numbers, then record their product on a Spinner Product Recording Sheet.

25 SUPER-FUN MATH SPINNER GAMES
Scholastic Professional Books, 1997

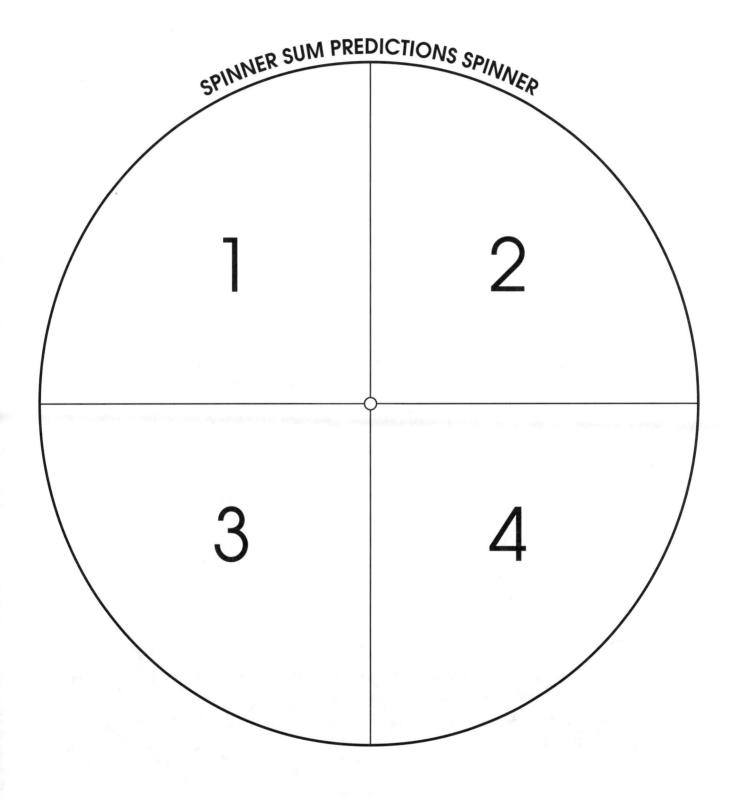

SPINNER SUM PREDICTIONS SPINNER

1   2

3   4

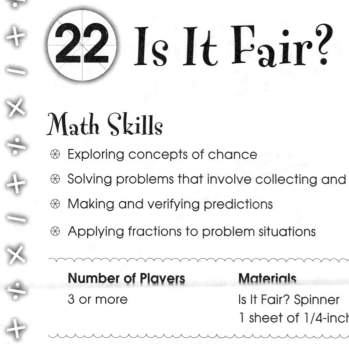

(22) Is It Fair?

Math Skills

- ⊗ Exploring concepts of chance
- ⊗ Solving problems that involve collecting and analyzing data
- ⊗ Making and verifying predictions
- ⊗ Applying fractions to problem situations

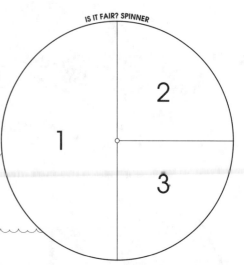

IS IT FAIR? SPINNER

Number of Players	Materials
3 or more	Is It Fair? Spinner
	1 sheet of 1/4-inch graph paper

HOW TO PLAY THE GAME

In this game, players try to predict the number of times they will spin the same number using the Is It Fair? Spinner. Have players make a graph-paper recording sheet with three columns labeled 1–3 and 30 rows labeled 1–30. After players have predicted which number they think they will spin most frequently—1, 2, or 3—have them spin 30 times and record their answers by coloring boxes on their chart. Next, have players identify the winning number by counting the colored boxes for each column. The player(s) who predicted the winning number correctly wins.

QUESTIONS TO EXPLORE

- ⊗ Were the results of this experiment the same as your predictions? Why do you think?
- ⊗ Do you think that all the groups will have the same results? Why?
- ⊗ Was this a fair game? Think about the spinner and the probability of spinning each number in terms of fractions. For example, the probability of spinning 1 is 1/2 because the number 1 takes up one half of the spinner.
- ⊗ How can we make this a fair game?

VARIATIONS AND EXTENSIONS

1. Compare your results with those of other players. Were they the same for each of you? Why or why not? What was the average answer?

2. Use the Is It Fair? Spinner to play Spinner Sum Predictions (p. 72). How does this spinner affect the results?

25 SUPER-FUN MATH SPINNER GAMES
Scholastic Professional Books, 1997

22 Is It Fair? Spinner

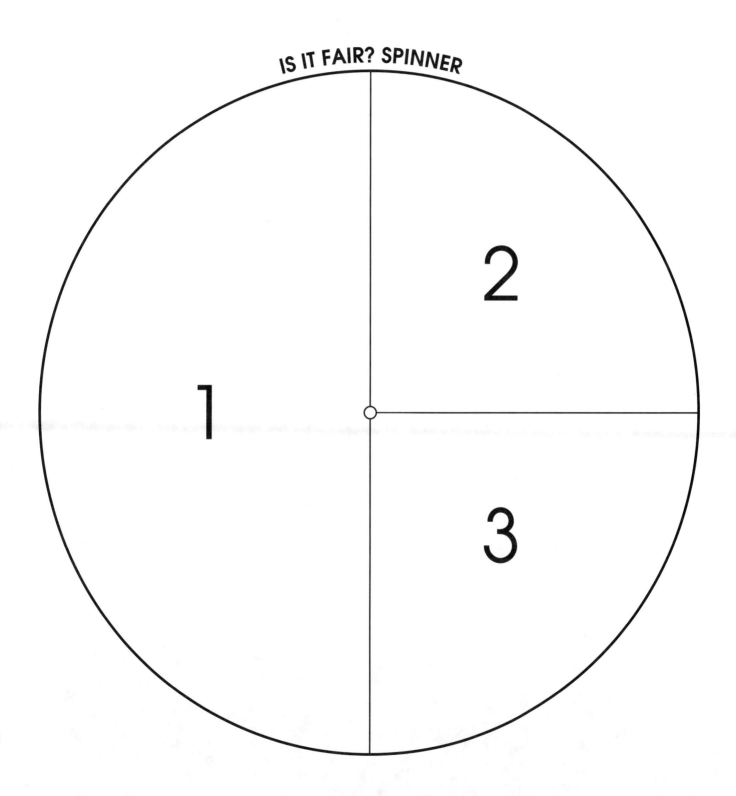

IS IT FAIR? SPINNER

2

1

3

Fractions
and
Decimals

(23) Money Exchange

Math Skills

⊗ Understanding our numeration system by relating counting, grouping, and place-value concepts

⊗ Developing an understanding of regrouping in addition and subtraction by using money

⊗ Understanding our monetary system

Number of Players	Materials
2–4 players	1 Money Exchange Game Board per player
	25 pennies
	20 nickels
	20 dimes
	10 quarters
	Money Exchange Spinner

MONEY EXCHANGE SPINNER

Add 3 pennies. | Subtract 4 pennies.
Add 1 penny. | Add 1 nickel and 1 penny.
Subtract 3 pennies. | Add 1 dime.
Add 1 nickel. | Subtract 1 nickel and 1 penny.

HOW TO PLAY THE GAME

The goal of the game is to be the first player to get 1 quarter. Players start with a blank board and then take turns spinning the spinner and adding or removing the number of coins indicated. The coins are placed in the appropriate columns. For example, if the spinner stops at "Add 3 pennies," the player places 3 pennies in the Pennies column of the game board. If the player spins "Subtract 3 pennies," he must remove 3 pennies from the board. If there are not enough pennies on the game board, coins must be exchanged for pennies (i.e., 1 nickel for 5 pennies). Only available money can be subtracted. When a player finally collects 5 pennies, he exchanges them for 1 nickel. If the player gets 2 nickels or 1 nickel and 5 pennies, they may be exchanged for 1 dime. Likewise, 2 dimes and 1 nickel can be exchanged for 1 quarter. The first player to collect 25 cents and exchange them for 1 quarter, wins the game.

QUESTIONS TO EXPLORE

⊗ What did you learn about our monetary system while playing this game?

VARIATIONS AND EXTENSIONS

1. Change the goal of the game so that players aim to get 3 quarters.
2. Have students write addition or subtraction sentences to describe their moves on the game board.

78

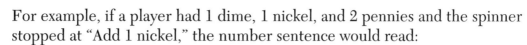

For example, if a player had 1 dime, 1 nickel, and 2 pennies and the spinner stopped at "Add 1 nickel," the number sentence would read:

$$17 ¢$$
$$\underline{+ 5 ¢}$$
$$22 ¢$$

3. Change the game by having students create a Money Exchange Game Board with columns for pennies, dimes, and dollars. This game board represents our base-ten number system.

4. Play the Reverse Money Exchange game. Here the goal of the game is to subtract money until the game board is emptied of all coins. Every time the spinner lands on a space that asks players to add, they would subtract instead. Begin the game with two quarters.

> For example, if the spinner stops at "Subtract 4 Pennies," the player must first exchange 1 of the quarters for 1 dime, 2 nickels, and 5 pennies. Then she would have to remove 4 pennies.

> Players keep exchanging quarters for dimes and pennies until all the coins are gone. The first player with an empty board wins.

MONEY EXCHANGE GAME BOARD

Quarters	Dimes	Nickels	Pennies

25 SUPER-FUN MATH SPINNER GAMES
Scholastic Professional Books, 1997

(23) Money Exchange Spinner

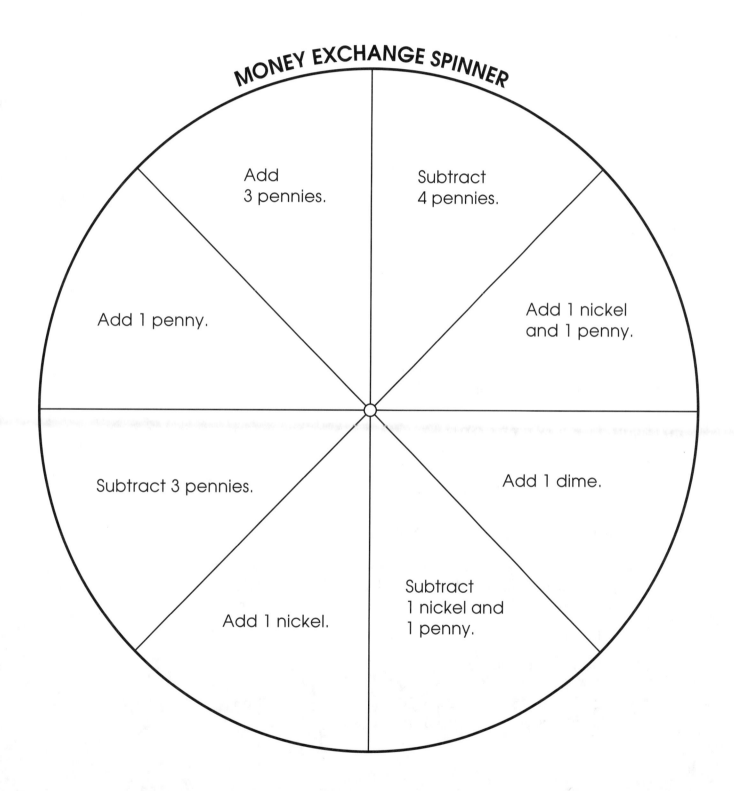

MONEY EXCHANGE SPINNER

Add
3 pennies.

Subtract
4 pennies.

Add 1 penny.

Add 1 nickel
and 1 penny.

Subtract 3 pennies.

Add 1 dime.

Add 1 nickel.

Subtract
1 nickel and
1 penny.

24 Fractional Spin

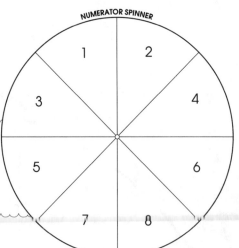

Math Skills

⊗ Naming and comparing fractions

Number of Players	Materials
2–4 players	Denominator Spinner
	Numerator Spinner
	Fractional Spin Recording Sheet

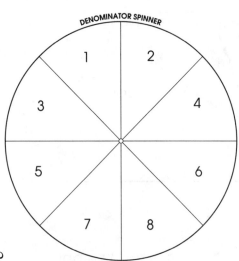

HOW TO PLAY THE GAME

The goal of the game is to have the most fractions circled on the recording sheet. Each player takes a turn spinning both the Denominator and Numerator Spinners. Players record their fraction in each box of the recording sheet. The player with the greatest fraction for the round circles the fraction on his chart. After 25 rounds, when the recording sheet is filled in, the player with the most fractions circled wins.

QUESTIONS TO EXPLORE

⊗ Can you think of other ways to play this game?
⊗ Which fractions that were formed are greater than 1?

VARIATIONS AND EXTENSIONS

1. Play the Fractions of 100 game. Players spin both spinners and combine the numbers selected to make a fraction that is less than 1. Players find that fraction of 100 and add it to their score. The first player whose score totals 150 or more is the winner.

   Example:

   If the player spins:

1	5	1/5 of 100	=	20
2	6	2/6 of 100	=	33 1/3
2	8	2/8 of 100	=	25

25 SUPER-FUN MATH SPINNER GAMES
Scholastic Professional Books, 1997

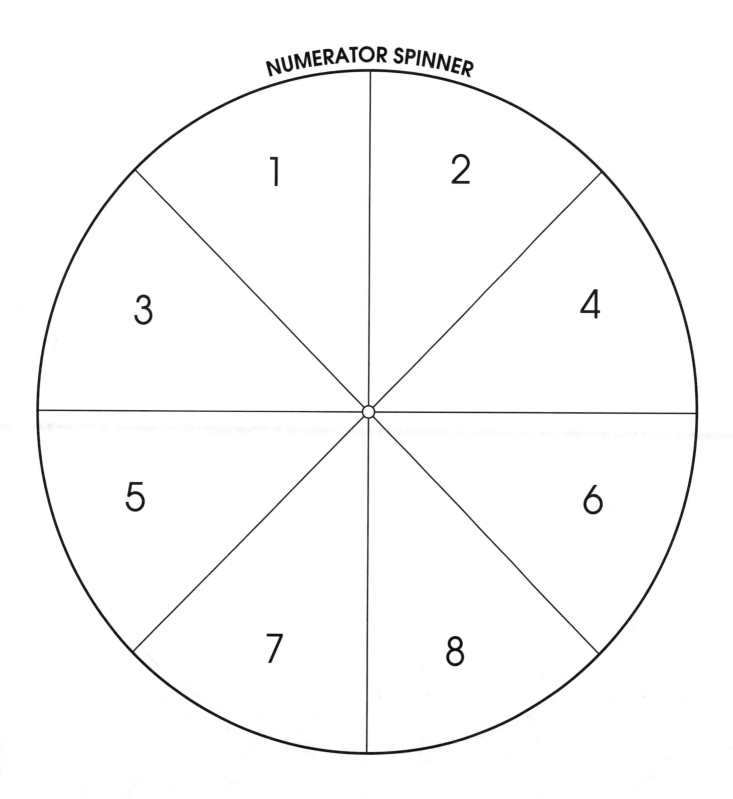

NUMERATOR SPINNER

Denominator Spinner

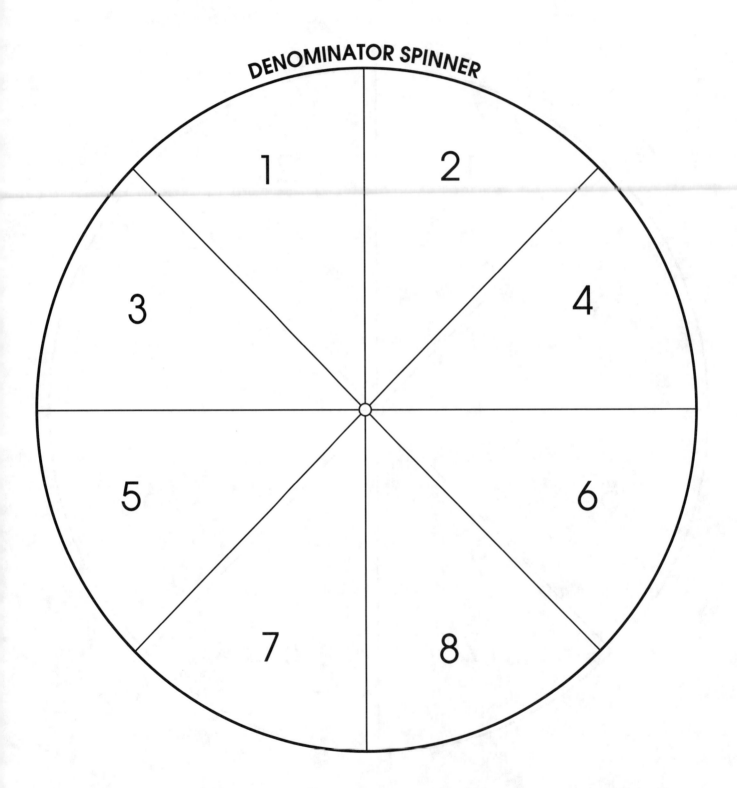

DENOMINATOR SPINNER

1   2

3   4

5   6

7   8

25 SUPER-FUN MATH SPINNER GAMES
Scholastic Professional Books, 1997

FRACTIONAL SPIN RECORDING SHEET

(25) Fractional Bingo

Math Skills

⊗ Naming and comparing fractions

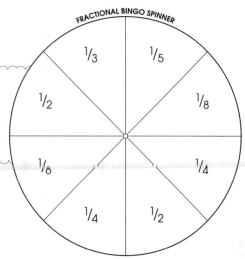

FRACTIONAL BINGO SPINNER

Number of Players	Materials
2–4	Fractional Bingo Spinner
	1 Fractional Bingo Card per player
	50 markers

HOW TO PLAY THE GAME

The goal of the game is to be the first player to cover any row either horizontally, vertically, or diagonally on the Fractional Bingo Card. Each player customizes his or her card by filling the blank spaces with illustrated representations of 3 of the following fractions: 1/2, 1/3, 1/4, 1/5, 1/6, or 1/8. Then players put a marker on the X and play begins. Each player takes a turn spinning the Fractional Bingo Spinner. Then they look to their bingo card to see where they have an illustration that represents the chosen fraction, and they cover that illustration with a marker. While a fraction may appear in a few places on the card, players may only place a marker in one box per spin. Should a player spin the same fraction more than once, he or she may continue placing markers in boxes with that fraction until they are all covered. Once they are all covered, however, and the player spins the same fraction again, he or she must skip a turn. The first player to fill a row with markers either horizontally, vertically, or diagonally is the winner.

QUESTIONS TO EXPLORE

⊗ What strategies did you use to customize your bingo card?

VARIATIONS AND EXTENSIONS

1. In addition to having students customize their bingo cards, you can have them create their own fractional spinners for practice with other fractions.

25 SUPER-FUN MATH SPINNER GAMES
Scholastic Professional Books, 1997

(25) Fractional Bingo Spinner

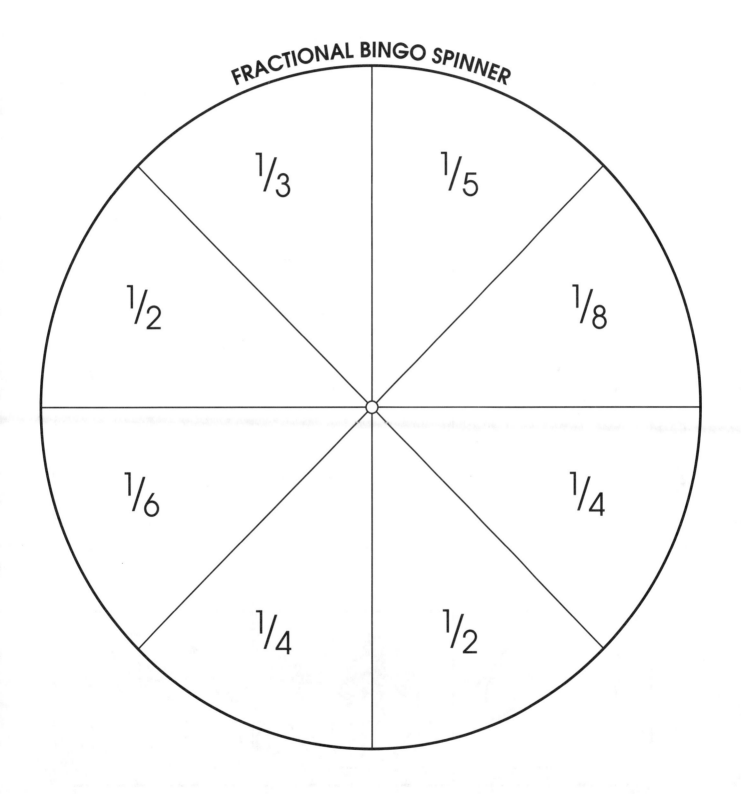

FRACTIONAL BINGO SPINNER

1/3   1/5

1/2   1/8

1/6   1/4

1/4   1/2

FRACTIONAL BINGO CARD

25 SUPER-FUN MATH SPINNER GAMES
Scholastic Professional Books, 1997

Spinner Templates

Spinner with Numbers 0-9

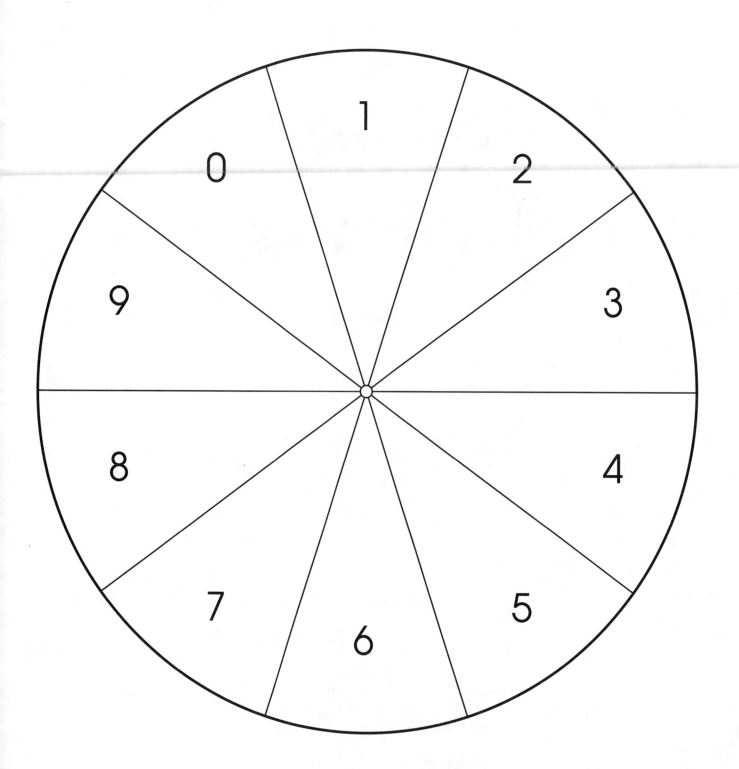

25 SUPER-FUN MATH SPINNER GAMES
Scholastic Professional Books, 1997

Spinner with Numbers 1-9

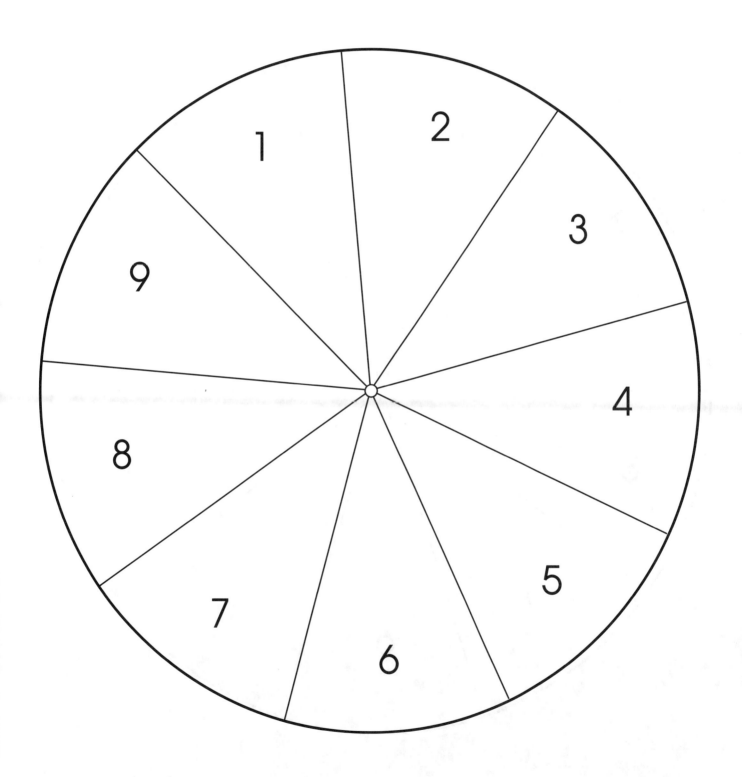

Spinner with Numbers 1-10

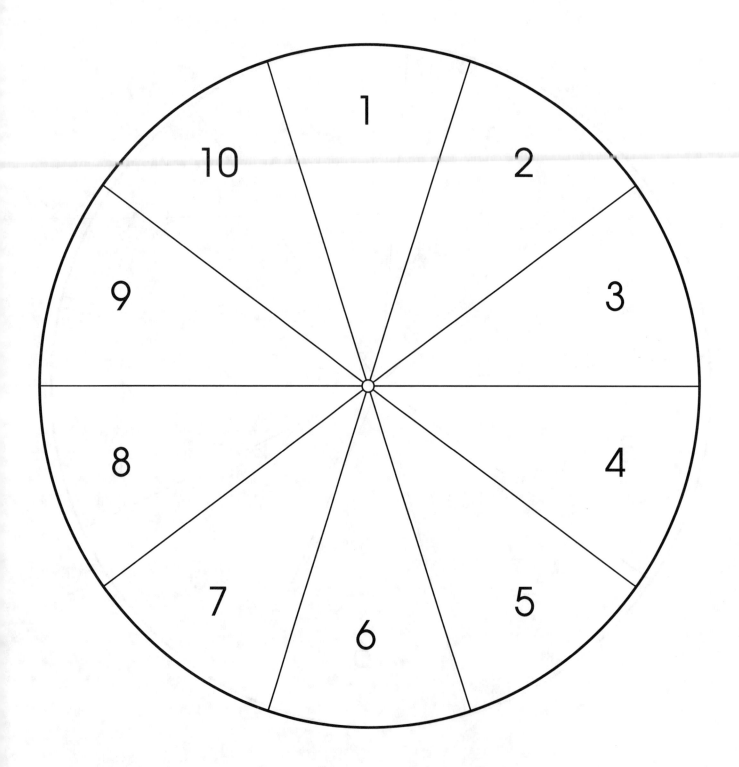

25 SUPER-FUN MATH SPINNER GAMES
Scholastic Professional Books, 1997

Blank Spinner

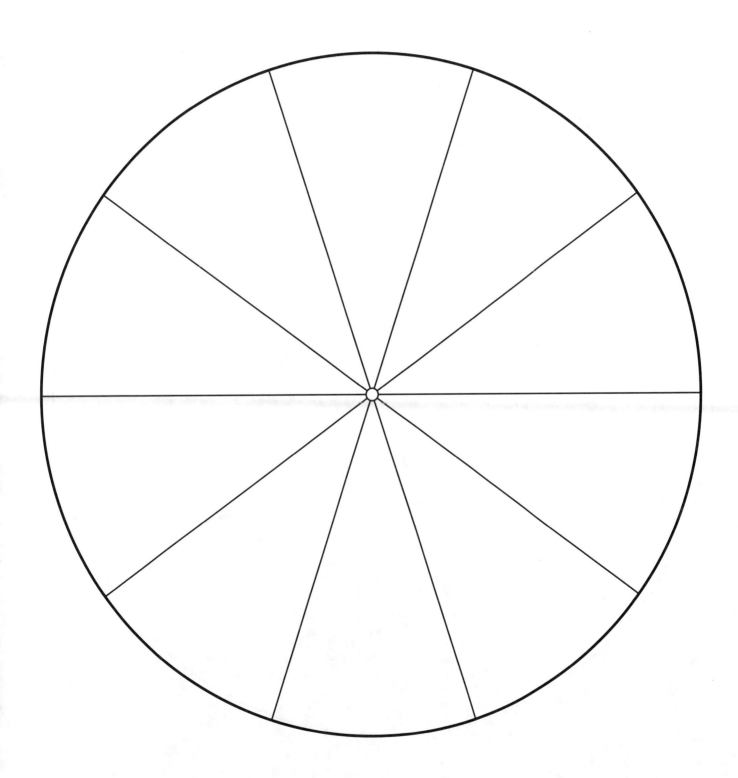

Blank Spinner

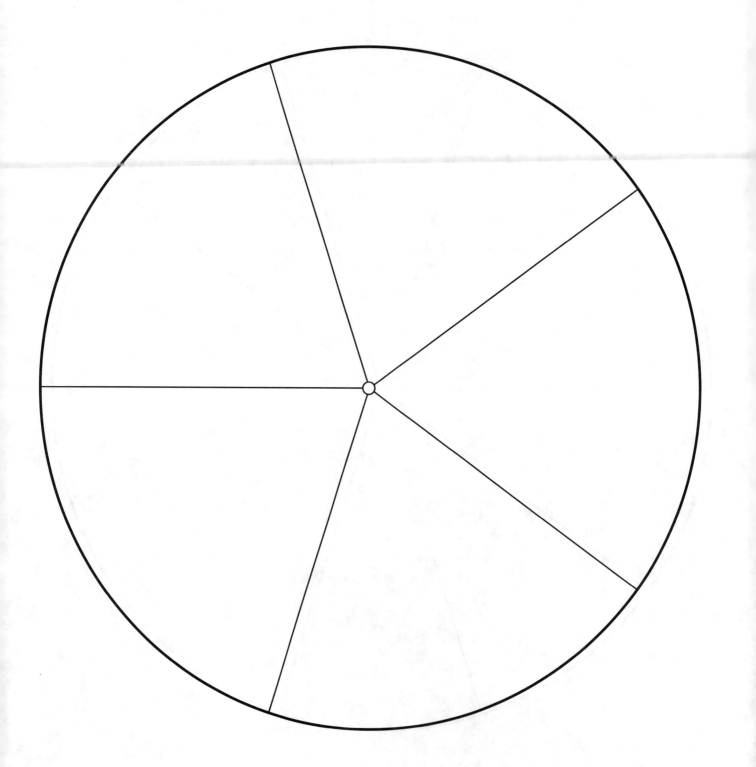

25 SUPER-FUN MATH SPINNER GAMES
Scholastic Professional Books, 1997

Spinner Arrows

Make a copy of this page and paste it to oaktag. Then, color and cut out the spinner arrows and attach them to the paper clip spinner arms with tape.

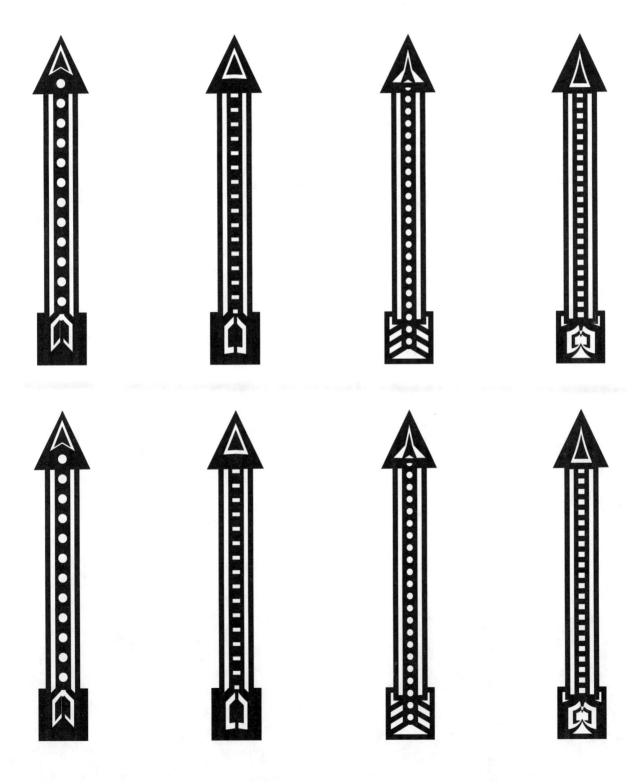